Praise for Hungry is a Mighty Fine Sauce

"You are going to love this cookbook. Not only do you get great recipes that even the pickiest of men, like mine, will love but you get great stories. Who doesn't love to pick up a cookbook and look through the recipes and read fun stories by the author? Shellie has been one of my favorite people for years, and she just made me *happy happy happy* with this cookbook. She shares things in such a fun way. I can just see her face in my mind telling the stories as I read them. She is a beautiful person with incredible stories to tell. A 'real' storyteller!"

—Miss Kay Robertson of A&E's *Duck Dynasty*

"I have had the good fortune to swap biscuits at the table with the Queen of Us All, and I can attest that everything Shellie says in these pages is the Gospel Truth, or at least a pretty good representation of it. What I can't figure out is how a woman who can cook this good can stay so skinny (*Bless her heart. . .*and Southerners will understand that). Maybe it's because the one thing Shellie does better than cooking is swapping stories. I'm getting a copy of *Hungry is a Mighty Fine Sauce* for each of my four grown Yankee children. Git you a copy and eat up!"

—Karen Spears Zacharias, Author of *Burdy*

"Did you ever meet a new friend who, in an instant, made you feel as if you've known her for years? Whose welcoming presence makes you want to relax, kick off your shoes, and linger? Who inspires you to think deeply and laugh out loud? Now imagine that woman also loves to cook and invites you to drop by for supper (or lunch, or breakfast, or dessert. . . .) That is how you'll feel reading Shellie's hilarious, uplifting stories and mouth-watering recipes in *Hungry is a Mighty Fine Sauce*. Like you've just spent time with a warm, funny friend surrounded by fabulous, home-cooked food. Doesn't get much better than that, my friends."

—Becky Johnson, Coauthor (with her daughter, Rachel Randolph)
of *We Laugh, We Cry, We Cook* and *Nourished:*
A Search for Health, Happiness and a Full Night's Sleep

"Hilarious sassy southern stories tucked between can't-wait-to-try-this recipes. . .some tried and true southern fare, others invented by Shellie herself, a true culinary artist. This girl knows *good* y'all. Particularly when it comes to what she calls the holy trinity of Southern cooking: chopped onion, bell pepper, and celery. I reckon the Trinity is the secret sauce of Shellie's Perfect Pea Topping Relish and a dozen other yumdillyicious marvels that make you want to slap your mama (one of Shellie's delightful colloquialisms I just might have to borrow!). A must-have for all belles and belle-wannabes!"

—Debora M. Coty, Humorist, Speaker,
and Author of the *Too Blessed to be Stressed Cookbook*

"As a new wife and cook, I love how Mrs. Shellie keeps it real and simple while sharing her best cooking secrets with me!"

—Mary Kate Eacham Robertson,
Wife of the young and beardless John Luke Robertson of A&E's *Duck Dynasty*

"With her trademark southern humor and wit, Shellie Rushing Tomlinson delivers a cookbook that will warm both your heart and your appetite. You might even forget to cook the delicious recipes as you'll get caught up in the stories, anecdotes, and beauty of the book itself. But don't forget to cook, because Shellie brings us the best of her own kitchen and farm in this collection of recipes and stories. If you get one cookbook this year, let it be this one!"

—Patti Callahan Henry,
New York Times bestselling author of *The Idea of Love*

"We southerners love our stories and our food; we'll eat and talk most anywhere, but we do a fine job of bringing the two together over a crowded dinner table. In *Hungry is a Mighty Fine Sauce*, Shellie Tomlinson takes food and stories to a whole NEW level. It's filled with funny stories about Shellie's family and friends. Who doesn't love the story about Lady, the holy ghost dog, and then there's one about Shellie, her BFF Rhonda, and a practical joke that occurred at 25,000 feet. With all those great stories there is also a host of yummy recipes, like Shellie's Mexican Lasagna, Mama's Chicken and Dressing, Holiday Hurt Yourself Bread, and Aunt Judy's Banana Nut Cake. And y'all, this is my favorite part—these recipes have ingredients I can find in my pantry and at my local grocery store. No obscure roots or unheard-of spice that you can only find in stores where they sell unicorn horns and fairy dust. Oh and the pictures—goodness, the pictures are gorgeous. Shellie combines flat out funny stories with mouthwatering recipes, and that makes this one of my favorite cookbooks—ever. I know what I'm getting everyone on my Christmas list this year!"

—Mary R Snyder, Author of *God, Grace & Girlfriends:*
Adventures in Faith and Friendship and *Authentic Girlfriends:*
Real Women Finding Real Faith

Hungry is a MIGHTY FINE Sauce

RECIPES & RAMBLINGS FROM
The Belle of All Things Southern

THE STORYTELLING COOK
Shellie Rushing Tomlinson

SHILOH RUN ▲ PRESS
An Imprint of Barbour Publishing, Inc.

Print ISBN 978-1-63409-782-6

eBook Editions:
Adobe Digital Edition (.epub) 978-1-68322-024-4
Kindle and MobiPocket Edition (.prc) 978-1-68322-025-1

The author is represented by and this book is published in association with the literary agency of WordServe Literary Group, Ltd., www.wordserveliterary.com

Published by Shiloh Run Press, an imprint of Barbour Publishing, Inc., P.O. Box 719, Uhrichsville, Ohio 44683, www.shilohrunpress.com.

Our mission is to publish and distribute inspirational products offering exceptional value and biblical encouragement to the masses.

Member of the
Evangelical Christian
Publishers Association

Printed in China.

Dedication

To Mama with love. This cookbook is dedicated to the
food of my raising and the hands that prepared it.
I'd rather put my feet under your table and swap stories
with family and friends than place them under the
most celebrated five-star restaurant around.
And to my treasured readers and radio listeners,
this cookbook exists because you embraced my
recipes based on that same style of down-home cooking,
and you beat the drums to see them compiled between
two covers. Thank you for the friendship and the support.
Now, put your feet under my table, and let's chat.

Hugs,

Shellie

Contents

Introduction

Hello, folks. Let's chat. I've been using those four words for more than a dozen years now to launch into a story with my readers and radio listeners. Sometimes my stories have a logical conclusion, and sometimes they even have a take-away message, but more often than not it's just me telling another one on my friends and family or opining on current events. Take nekked people. It's a given, if nekked news has broken out anywhere on the globe, I'm going to work it into the conversation, mostly because saying the word *nekked* makes me laugh, and for the life of me, I don't understand the fascination with going au naturel.

In the middle of all this storytelling, you can find me sharing recipes, be it hand-me-downs from my lineage of stellar southern cooks, new dishes sent in by my readers, or slap-your-mama good ideas I've picked up during my travels as I flit around the country in my official role as the Belle of All Things Southern. Two things—first, I realize that name sounds all prissy and everything, but anyone can get themselves a title. Remind me to tell y'all how I got mine. And two, I'm certainly not suggesting that you actually slap your mama. That's simply the southern way of saying something is dangerously delicious.

Over the years, my readers and radio listeners have embraced my style of good food made easy and asked me to do a cookbook. My initial response to these continuing requests was to tuck a number of recipes into my last two nonfiction humor books, *Suck Your Stomach In and Put Some Color On* and *Sue Ellen's Girl Ain't Fat, She Just Weighs Heavy*. I thought this would satisfy the recipe lovers, but no siree, they wanted more, and I don't mean maybe! I'm not the sharpest knife in the drawer, but when readers began telling me they were printing all my recipes off from the website and binding them to give away as gifts, I said to myself, "Self, we need to do a cookbook!" Yeah, I'm smart like that.

And speaking of smart, forgive me, but I'm about to launch straight into proud mama mode. My daughter, Jessica Maher, is the su- perpopular food blogger behind KitchenBelle- icious.com. I'm pleased to be able to introduce Jessica and some of her recipes in these pages, too! And blessings on top of blessings, my daughter-in-law, Carey Tomlinson, captured these beautiful images for me.

All that said, it's time to get some food on the table. Seeing as how I believe that all the best recipes come with a story, there's only one thing left to say. Have a seat, folks, and let's chat.

1

CASSEROLES, SLOW-COOKER DINNERS, AND ONE-DISH MEALS

FEEDING THE FUNNY FARM

It means, "I love you. And I am sorry for what you are going through and I will share as much of your burden as I can." And maybe potato salad is a better way of saying it.

WILL D. CAMPBELL

My family has an all-for-one-and-one-for-all policy when it comes to visiting one another in the hospital. We've been known to take over a waiting room at a moment's notice and hold the fort for the duration of a loved one's stay. This can't be easy on the other folks forced to share the waiting area with us, but in our defense, we aren't at all exclusive. Should you find yourself in the vicinity, you're welcome to our snacks, and you're free to join the conversation, but good luck getting the floor. Do you remember jumping rope in grade school and how tricky it was to learn how to time your entrance when someone else was swinging the rope without getting clotheslined? Excellent. You'll need to draw on that skill should you decide to enter the conversational fray.

One of our last big get-togethers was held on Mama's behalf. She, who is affectionately known in this family as the Queen of Us All, drew quite the impressive gathering for her latest back surgery, and boy did we swap some stories that day! One of my author friends, Karen Spears Zacharias, had recently written a perfectly hilarious piece about childbirth and cod liver oil on her blog, and I took great delight in sharing it with the assembled females. That's another one of our family idiosyncrasies: we women seriously enjoy telling our childbirth stories. By now we know one another's experiences by heart, but somehow or another they always get better in the retelling. I know that I personally spare no details with mine.

I like to say medical books will tell you the human female's gestation period is forty weeks, but they will not tell you that once the human female passes that date she will become open to all manner of suggestions as to how to get that baby out. Midway through my first pregnancy, my doctor told me to quit riding my bike lest it send me into labor. At nine months and two weeks, I took him up on that promise. He lied. All I got for my trouble was curious stares from the neighborhood kids, and I couldn't blame 'em. Can you picture a circus elephant balancing on a ball? Good. That will give you some idea of what those poor things were forced to witness.

The women in my family told me castor oil would do the trick. They lied, too. That stuff did a lot of things to my body all right. Nasty things. Everything in me turned loose—except that sweet baby.

But about the Queen. Before her surgery was over that day, we had enjoyed something between a family feud and a family reunion. As alluded to earlier, the only thing harder than getting the floor to share a story in my southern family is keeping it until you're through. Breathe and you'll forfeit your turn till the next round—unless you're willing to use force to retain your audience. Most of us are.

My friend Janis would totally get that. She's a southern girl whose ex-husband is an Iranian, but she swears he's not a terrorist or anything. His people are actually considered the less dangerous side of the family. Or, as her daughter Sara Jane has been known to say, "Don't mess with me. My family is half Iranian and half rednecks. The Iranian side will take you hostage. The redneck side will take you out!"

We resemble that.

Don't Be Crabby Casserole

You can stir up my Don't Be Crabby Casserole in the morning and stash it in the refrigerator before you join the boisterous group at the hospital. Upon your return that evening, just pull it out, bake it, and serve it with a nice green salad for one satisfying meal.

1 loaf french bread, cubed (6 to 8 cups)

1 bunch green onions, sliced

2 cups grated swiss cheese (may substitute mozzarella)

16 ounces fresh crabmeat

4 eggs

3 cups milk

1 teaspoon dry mustard

1 teaspoon Tony Chachere's Original Creole Seasoning

Salt and pepper to taste

Grated cheese for topping

Pull french bread into bite-size pieces and layer in ungreased 9x13 casserole dish. Top with half of sliced green onions, grated cheese, and fresh crabmeat. Repeat.

Beat eggs and milk in small bowl. Flavor with seasonings and pour across top of casserole layers. Bake uncovered at 325 degrees for 90 minutes. When knife inserted into center of dish comes out clean, sprinkle on a little more cheese and slide dish back into oven until cheese melts. Enjoy!

Spicy Stuffed Peppers

Now, most of us have had stuffed peppers before. This is the same process. Nothing earth-shattering here. I'm just sharing the flavors and cooking process I prefer. You can add rice to your stuffing or serve it on the side. Either way, it's mighty good eating!

8 large bell peppers (I like to use yellow, orange, red, and green for a beautiful presentation!)

1 small white onion, minced

5 to 6 jalapeño peppers, minced

½ pound hot pork sausage

½ pound ground beef

2 tablespoons olive oil

1 clove garlic, minced

1 teaspoon cilantro

1 teaspoon cumin

1 teaspoon chili powder

1 teaspoon oregano

Salt and pepper to taste

4 ounces mozzarella cheese, grated

4 ounces Monterey Jack cheese, grated

Wash and prepare peppers by slicing off tops and removing seeds and membranes. Mince onion and jalapeño peppers.

Brown sausage and ground beef in olive oil with minced onion. Drain fat. Season with minced garlic, cilantro, cumin, chili powder, oregano, and salt and pepper to taste. Stir in cheeses.

Stuff bell peppers and bake at 350 degrees for 30 to 45 minutes. Enjoy!

Belle Tip:

If you're in a superbig hurry, you can steam your peppers in a bag in the microwave for a few minutes to cut down on the cooking time.

SAUSAGE GUMBO BAKE

Families are like gumbos, full of a little bit of everything—much like my Sausage Gumbo Bake. It's a scrumpdillyicious dish to take to an ailing relative or to serve the next hungry group that gathers at your own house, and there's something in this recipe for everybody!

½ (10 ounce) bag frozen diced green peppers and onions

3 tablespoons butter for sautéing

1 pound fully cooked smoked sausage, cut into ¼-inch slices

¼ cup Tony Chachere's Creole Instant Roux mix

1 (10 ounce) can Ro-Tel original diced tomatoes and green chilies

32 ounces chicken broth

1 (16 ounce) package frozen okra

1 cup uncooked rice

3 tablespoons butter, melted

2 cloves garlic, minced

1 teaspoon Cajun seasoning

2 teaspoons dried parsley

1 (12 ounce) loaf frozen french bread, open and cut into ½-inch slices

Sauté diced peppers and onions in butter. In a separate skillet, brown sausage and stir in instant roux mix. (I find this roux mix in the seasoning department of our grocery store, and it can also be purchased online. If you can't find it or you want to make your own gravy, just make a nice brown roux by stirring in a tablespoon or so of flour into your sausage drippings. Let it cook until it's dark brown. Around here we say "next door to burnt." Add a few cups of cold water and continue to stir, loosening the sausage from the bottom of your skillet. Heat to boiling then reduce heat and simmer. You've got gravy! Note: if you decide to make gravy instead of using the roux mix, cut down on the chicken broth by roughly the same amount of water you use in the gravy.)

If you make your own roux, return sausage to roux and add diced peppers and onions. Cook over low heat a couple of minutes before adding tomatoes, chicken broth, frozen okra, rice, and butter. Season with minced garlic and Cajun seasoning. Heat to boiling. Then remove from heat and pour gumbo into 9x13 baking dish. Stir in dried parsley. Bake, covered, at 350 degrees for 50 to 60 minutes. Uncover, then top with bread slices and bake another 10 minutes while you pour the sweet tea.

All I need today is a little bit of sweet tea and a whole lot of Jesus.

CROCK-POT FIESTA

My Crock-Pot Fiesta is a great make-ahead meal. If you're in a really big hurry, it's okay to put the onions and chicken breasts directly into your Crock-Pot. However, if you can spare a couple of minutes to sear your chicken in a hot skillet on the stove, you'll create a ton of extra flavor and your chicken won't look all white and pasty. Who wants that?

1 onion, diced

1 tablespoon extra virgin olive oil

2 tablespoons butter

3 cloves garlic, minced

1 pound chicken breasts

1 teaspoon Cajun seasoning

1 tablespoon Worcestershire sauce

1 cup chicken broth

1 (15 ounce) can diced tomatoes

1 (15 ounce) can black beans

1 cup frozen corn

1 teaspoon cumin

1 teaspoon cayenne pepper

1 teaspoon hot sauce

Salt and pepper to taste

2 to 4 cups cooked rice

Cilantro and green onions for topping

Sauté diced onion in olive oil and butter until translucent. Add minced garlic and cook for no more than a minute. Transfer onion and garlic to slow cooker. Season chicken breasts with Cajun seasoning and Worcestershire sauce. Brown in skillet 3 minutes on both sides and transfer to slow cooker.

Deglaze skillet with chicken broth and add drippings to slow cooker. Add tomatoes, black beans, corn, seasonings, and hot sauce. Cook 6 to 8 hours on low or 3 to 4 hours on high. Remove chicken, shred, and return to slow cooker. Serve over hot, fluffy rice, and top with chopped cilantro and green onions.

BELLE TIP:
You can also make a tasty soup from this recipe by adding more chicken broth!

Cajun Chow Mein

This dish has been in our family for as long as I can remember. When I was a little girl, I thought the name sounded so adventurous compared to our standard country fare. Who knew Mama had just found another name for meat and taters? The only change I've made to Mama's chow mein is to replace the canned soup with my own basic white sauce. If you prefer to use cream of mushroom, knock yourself out. I won't tell the foodies.

1 small onion, diced
1 small bell pepper, diced
1 green pepper, diced
2 stalks celery, diced
4 tablespoons butter
1 pound ground beef
2 cups water
1 cup uncooked rice
1 (10 ounce) can Ro-Tel tomatoes
Dash Worcestershire sauce
Dash hot sauce
1 teaspoon Cajun seasoning
1 small carton fresh sliced mushrooms
Salt and pepper to taste

WHITE SAUCE:
2 tablespoons butter
2 tablespoons flour
1 cup milk

Sauté onion, peppers, and celery in butter until soft and onions are clear. Brown ground beef, drain off fat, and transfer with veggies to large casserole dish sprayed with cooking spray.

Prepare white sauce in skillet by melting butter and stirring in flour. Cook 3 to 4 minutes on low before adding milk. Simmer another 2 to 3 minutes. Stir white sauce into beef and veggies along with 2 cups water, uncooked rice, and Ro-Tel tomatoes. Add Worcestershire sauce, hot sauce, and seasonings.

Cook 30 to 45 minutes at 350 degrees, adding mushrooms in the last 5 to 10 minutes. Stir occasionally to prevent any sticking. You may need to add a little water if dish begins to dry out. When your rice is ready, the dish is ready!

*M*y sisters and I considered it a privilege to nurse Mama as she recovered from that previously mentioned back surgery. It was only right seeing as how the Queen of Us All has spent her entire life tending to anyone within tending distance—whether they wanted to be tended to or not. (But that's another story.)

For me, one of the more endearing aspects of all this "Mama tending" was listening to Mama's phone conversations with her sisters, a group of darlings I fondly call the Golden Girls. One day Mama was having her phone therapy with her sisters while I was working nearby on my laptop. She and Judy Lynn (the youngest Golden Girl) had already straightened out one half of the world. Mama and Aunt Marleta (Golden Girl number three) were now having a go at the other half. I knew they had started with Uncle Stan's deteriorating health. Uncle Stan is Aunt Marleta's husband of more than fifty years. He's still at home, but he's on oxygen and they keep increasing his levels. I hated hearing that, but I must've somewhat zoned out on my work because Mama's worry voice suddenly broke into my thoughts.

"Um, um, um," Mama was saying. "He's not long for this world."

Concerned and curious, I got Mama's attention and made a *Who are you talking about?* gesture.

Mama spoke to me over the receiver, "Stanley."

"Are you still talking to Aunt Marleta?" I asked incredulously. Mama nodded in affirmation. "And you're telling her that her husband is dying?"

"Just a minute," Mama said into the phone before turning back to me. "Yes, Shellie. Marleta knows."

Well, okay then.

That's the way it is with my people; you always know where you stand. For further illustration, that same day I witnessed another of my favorite sources of parental entertainment, this being the humorous exchanges between the Queen of Us All and her long-suffering King. To be fair, the long-suffering title should be up for grabs between those two. Papa has made a hobby out of aggravating Mama. That particular afternoon the Queen was nagging, I mean *reminding* Papa, for the umpteenth dozen time about something he'd been promising to do but hadn't gotten around to, when Papa froze in his tracks and calmly met her gaze.

"Look-a-here," he said, "do you know who you're talking to?"

Ruh-roh! I sensed trouble. The Queen, however, was unperturbed.

"I sure do," she said. "I'm talking to you, Ed Rushing." I held my breath in the brief silence that followed, until Papa started grinning so big his eyes disappeared. With Papa, that's always a sign there's a joke straight ahead.

"All righty then," he said. "I was just making sure you knew."

As it was, I shouldn't have been surprised to hear Mama and Aunt Marleta openly discussing how much longer Uncle Stan has before he claims his eternal reward. Turns out, that was nothing. Shortly after that phone chat, Mama's sister and brother-in-law came to check on her, and the deadly conversation continued with Uncle Stan sitting in the same room. Granted, his hearing isn't so good and he did have the TV up sky-high, and his oxygen tank can be noisy, but still.

Just about the time I decided he couldn't hear their morbid conversation, and for that we could be grateful, Uncle Stan proved me wrong. Aunt Marleta was telling Mama how she'd recently sent Uncle Stan's military uniform to the cleaners so it would be, well. . .*ready* (her words), when her man spoke up to register his opinion.

"That's what you know, 'Leta," Uncle Stan said. "That suit doesn't even fit me anymore." His beloved shrugged off that news with her own just-the-facts announcement, "Don't worry about that none, Stanley. They'll slip your arms through the sleeves, slit that jacket down the back, and no one will ever be the wiser."

Uncle Stan took this information in with a solemn expression and returned to his TV program.

That's when Aunt Marleta told me how she was thinking about keeping his body around after he passed. I mentioned that was a felony, but Aunt Marleta said she felt like it would be worth it to keep his check coming. She said there are things a person can shake on the body so it doesn't smell. She was joking.

I think.

Of course, Aunt Marleta isn't just planning Uncle Stan's funeral. She went on to tell me that she's working on the details of her own big day. She wants her face turned toward the audience before rigor mortis sets in, because it is so much more attractive than staring up at the ceiling. (Please tell me my people aren't the only people around who refer to a funeral as their "big day" and those gathered to pay respects as their "audience.")

Aunt Marleta also said she would prefer to have one hand resting on the side of the coffin. Don't ask me. I guess she wants to give the impression that she could change her mind and climb out at any minute.

I left the room and made a couple of calls to my sisters. "Here's the thing," I told them. "Our family is either extremely well adjusted when it comes to death and dying, or we are sick."

Sometimes it's a mighty fine line.

FETA CHEESE FRITTATA WITH MUSHROOMS

I was surveying my fridge one evening when I noted that I had a dozen eggs that had been with me awhile and a pound of fresh mushrooms that were close to perishing. The challenge, as I saw it, was to use them as the base for a delicious supper. Oh, I do love that sort of thing. A little more snooping revealed equal parts of Monterey Jack and feta. And that's when it hit me! I made a feta cheese frittata with mushrooms, and a star was born. It's a complete meal in itself.

2 tablespoons butter

2 tablespoons extra virgin olive oil

1 cup chopped onion, pepper, celery blend

1 pound mushrooms, sliced

1 tablespoon Worcestershire sauce

1 dozen eggs

4 ounces feta cheese

4 ounces Monterey Jack cheese

¼ cup milk

Salt and pepper

Cajun seasoning

Melt butter and stir in olive oil in skillet. Add chopped onion, pepper, and celery. (I love the frozen blend in the freezer department of the grocery store!) Sauté veggies until soft, then remove with slotted spoon. Add sliced mushrooms and 1 tablespoon Worcestershire sauce to butter and olive oil, and reduce. This will give the mushrooms added flavor.

Crack eggs into large mixing bowl and lightly blend with cheeses. Stir in milk. Season with salt, pepper, and Cajun seasoning. Drain mushrooms and return to skillet. Add egg mixture and veggies.

Bake in skillet at 375 degrees for 30 to 40 minutes or until eggs are set. If you have them, feel free to sprinkle some fresh herbs over the finished dish. (I used chopped parsley here.) Serve with a huge glass of cold milk. My Feta Cheese Frittata with Mushrooms is perfect for breakfast or supper. (If you're not from the southern states, you may call supper "dinner." It's your right to be wrong. ;-)

BELLE TIP:

Mama taught us girls to plan meals according to what might be about to perish in the pantry before running to the grocery store for new ingredients. If your potatoes have eyes, that's where you begin to build your meal. Why? Because if you aren't careful, you can throw more groceries out the back door than you can tote in the front! We call it "pantry cooking."

Chicken Spaghetti with Italian Dressing and Black Olives

This dish stays on my go-to list because it's delicious warm, but it also rocks the diners when it has been refrigerated overnight. Let's hear it for leftovers! Amen?

1 (1 pound) package vermicelli

1 red onion, chopped

1 stalk celery, chopped

2 tablespoons butter

1 pint fresh mushrooms

Rotisserie chicken

1 package dry Italian dressing

½ (24 ounce) bottle Italian dressing

1 (2.25 ounce) can sliced black olives

1 small (10.5 ounce) carton cherry tomatoes

1 bunch green onions, chopped

Salt and pepper to taste

Grated parmesan cheese

Prepare vermicelli according to package directions. Drain and set aside. Sauté onion and celery in butter until soft. Add mushrooms and cook another couple of minutes.

Meanwhile, take a rotisserie chicken, fresh from the grocery store, and pull it into bite-size pieces. Place drained vermicelli and prepped chicken in large serving bowl and toss with dry Italian dressing and bottled Italian dressing. Add sliced black olives, cherry tomatoes, and chopped green onions. Season to taste with salt and pepper, sprinkle with grated parmesan cheese, and toss well! Serve immediately or chilled from the fridge. Your group will thank you either way.

Shellie's Secret Recipe Chicken

The secret to this chicken dish is the artichoke hearts, but promise me you won't tell anyone up front, and it will be a surefire hit. Trust me, avowed anti-artichoke people will devour this if you catch 'em off guard!

8 boneless skinless chicken breast halves

2 tablespoons butter

2 (6 ounce) jars marinated artichoke hearts, drained

1 (4.5 ounce) can whole mushrooms, drained

½ cup chopped onion

2 cups chicken broth

⅓ cup flour

1½ teaspoons dried rosemary

Salt and pepper to taste

Brown chicken breasts in butter. Transfer to ungreased baking dish and save drippings in skillet. Chop artichoke hearts into bite-size pieces and layer over chicken. Top with mushrooms. Sauté chopped onion in reserved pan juices. When onion has become translucent, stir in chicken broth and flour. Season sauce with dried rosemary and salt and pepper to taste. Heat until thick, then pour over chicken breasts and bake at 350 degrees for 50 to 60 minutes or until chicken is tender. Serve over your favorite noodles.

Aunt Peggy's Chicken and Dumpling Casserole

This recipe is from my darling aunt Peggy (who is really my older cousin, but that's just family details). Although this dish was already delicious as it was, I tinkered with it a bit and substituted a white sauce for the canned soup. Don't worry about Aunt Peggy's feelings. She won't mind. Like the rest of the women in my family, we understand that a recipe is just a suggestion. Let's get cooking!

¼ cup (½ stick) butter

3 to 4 chicken breasts, roasted and shredded (or one store-bought rotisserie chicken)

½ teaspoon salt (or more to taste)

1 teaspoon black pepper

½ teaspoon dried sage

1 teaspoon minced garlic

2 cups Bisquick Baking Mix

2 cups whole milk

2 cups chicken broth

1 recipe Basic White Sauce (see p. 142) or 1 can cream of chicken soup

3 chicken bouillon cubes or 3 teaspoons chicken granules

Preheat oven to 350 degrees. Melt butter in 9x13 casserole dish. Layer shredded chicken over butter and sprinkle with salt, pepper, sage, and garlic. Now, this is important: *Do not stir.* Mix Bisquick with milk. Pour over chicken. Again, do not stir. Whisk chicken broth and 1 recipe of Basic White Sauce in mixing bowl. Stir in chicken bouillon cubes or chicken granules and pour slowly over Bisquick layer. You guessed it—no stirring. Bake 30 to 40 minutes at 350 degrees or until golden brown.

*A good marriage is like a casserole. . .only those
responsible for it really know what goes in it.*

ANONYMOUS

⊙ne of the stranger aspects of Mama's rehab from back surgery was the part a certain canine played in it. I speak here of Lady, the Holy Ghost Dog. After all this time, it still seems strange to type these words, but it is what it is: *my mother has an inside dog.* By that, I mean a dog is darkening Mama's door without threat of execution.

I understand if this announcement holds little surprise for you, dear reader, but then you know nothing of Mama's lifelong aversion to animals being allowed indoors. To those of us in her family, it is mind-boggling. I still find it hard to explain how strange it has been for us to watch Mama interact with her new four-legged friend. I can only liken it to the feeling we all had that year Les Miles and Nick Saban sat beside each other at the Heisman presentation acting like BFFs. It's hard to shake the feeling you've been had.

I wouldn't blame anyone for drawing the conclusion that pain meds were involved here, but the Holy Ghost Dog era actually predated the aforementioned back surgery. By the way, I call her Holy Ghost Dog because (a) she showed up right before Easter at my parents' church, convinced everyone she was homeless, and somehow charmed the folks into taking her in; and (b) only an act of God could have produced the scenario we've been witnessing ever since.

Mama christened the record-setting canine Lady Lucy, and somehow the little dachshund seemed to understand the fragile nature of her position from the get-go. My parents initially tried to act like they weren't smitten with the dog and the situation was temporary, but Lady Lucy was undaunted. If anything, it only seemed to increase her determination to bond.

Mama's pet peeve used to be the cats lounging on the back porch, but much to her delight, one of Lady's first official acts was to send those felines scampering to Papa's equipment shed. Score! My sisters and I are convinced Lady canvassed the premises and decided it was a fine place to put down roots, at any cost. She sits as still as a church mouse for her bath, and she allows great-grandchildren to tote her around without complaint.

The doctor said Mama's recovery would be slow and steady, and he was right, but it was soon obvious to everyone that Lady was acting as something of a therapist. God works in mysterious ways, all right. Sometimes He even uses Holy Ghost Dogs.

Buttermilk Shrimp Alfredo

One night I found some nice jumbo shrimp in the freezer, and my mind immediately went to shrimp alfredo. Unfortunately, I also noted that I didn't have any heavy cream for my homemade sauce. On the other hand, I did have some buttermilk, and my family does call me the Queen of Substitution. Turns out it was just what the Belle ordered!

1 pound jumbo shrimp

½ white onion, diced

½ green pepper, diced

2 tablespoons butter

1 (12 ounce) box fettuccine

2 tablespoons cornstarch

1 to 1½ cups buttermilk or heavy cream

1 teaspoon lemon juice

2 cloves garlic, minced

1 to 2 cups half-and-half

1 teaspoon seasoned salt

1 teaspoon cayenne pepper

1 tablespoon dried basil

Salt and pepper to taste

1 cup grated parmesan cheese

Wash and devein shrimp. Set aside. Sauté onions and peppers in butter while cooking fettuccine according to package directions. Combine cornstarch, buttermilk, and lemon juice in small bowl. Once onions and peppers soften, add shrimp and cook over medium heat for about 3 minutes until pink. Stir in cornstarch mixture and garlic. Add enough half-and-half to bring dish to your preferred consistency.

Season with seasoned salt, cayenne pepper, basil, salt, and pepper. Stir in grated parmesan and serve over cooked fettuccine (or your favorite pasta). We like to top ours with a little more parmesan at the table.

Mama's Chicken and Dressing

So, here's the thing. This recipe was originally printed in one of my first humor books. If you see it here, it means I successfully cajoled my editor into allowing me to include it in my first cookbook, too. Seriously, it just seemed like a crime to leave it out. Mama's Chicken and Dressing recipe is a treasured tradition in our family. Try it and see if it doesn't become golden in yours, too!

CORN BREAD:

2 cups self-rising cornmeal

⅓ cup self-rising flour

3 tablespoons bacon grease or shortening

2 eggs

1 to 2 tablespoons sugar

1¾ cups milk

DRESSING:

1 good-sized hen

1 pan corn bread

1 sleeve saltine crackers

1 white onion

4 stalks celery, chopped

5 eggs

Salt and pepper to taste

3 to 4 cups broth

Place good-sized hen in large kettle and cover it completely with water. Once water boils, turn down heat and cook hen on low until meat falls off bones. Remove hen from water and cool before deboning, making sure to save broth. It's priceless, and we'll use it in just a bit.

For corn bread, sift together cornmeal and flour. Cut in shortening (bacon grease is better if you have it). Add eggs, sugar, and milk. Stir well, pour into cast-iron skillet, and bake at 350 degrees for 30 minutes or until corn bread is brown.

For dressing, crumble corn bread into large bowl along with sleeve of crushed saltine crackers. Add chopped onion, celery, eggs, and salt and pepper to taste. Fold in deboned chicken meat. Spoon all ingredients into large buttered casserole dish. (It's important not to work your dressing too much; you'll make it dry.) Gradually add broth until ingredients are soft and mushy. This isn't an exact measurement, but you'll use about 3 to 4 cups of broth. Bake dressing about an hour at 350 degrees or until it begins to firm up and the edges get a nice crust, stirring maybe once. That's Mama's Chicken and Dressing.

My sister and I are so close that we finish each other's sentences and often wonder whose memories belong to whom.

SHANNON CELEBI

Once Mama had recovered enough to get up and about, I celebrated by throwing a luncheon for her and her sisters, the Golden Girls. The only thing that would've made the Sister-Sister party any better would've been if my own siblings had been able to come in to share the day with that venerated generation above us.

To know the Golden Girls is to love them. Ask my best buddy. Rhonda (a.k.a. Red) isn't kin to the sisters, but she appreciates their sassy southern ways as much as we do. In a roundabout way, this set her up just right for one of my twisted little jokes.

Red and I were visiting over coffee when she commented on how much help the Golden Girls had been during Mama's recovery from back surgery.

"Absolutely," I said. "I don't know what any of us would've done without her sisters."

Rhonda frowned. "And that reminds me of something I wanted to ask you. I know Marleta and Judy have been taking turns helping, but I haven't heard you say a word about your aunt Elaine."

I realized immediately that Red had completely forgotten that the oldest Golden Girl passed away a few years back! Quite naturally, I recognized just as quickly that I was being given an opportunity to have some fun at my friend's expense.

"Oh, Aunt Elaine hasn't been here once," I said.

"You're kidding!" Red was incredulous. "She hasn't helped at all?"

"Not at all," I repeated. "She hasn't lifted a finger."

This was entirely too much for Red, who was superhero quick to stand up for Mama suffering such an injustice from her oldest sister. "That's horrible, Shellie! Please tell me she has at least been calling your mama."

"Nope!"

Red's eyes widened. "And after all your mama has done to help everyone else in the family! I don't know what's gotten into your aunt Elaine."

All good things must come to an end. I figured the time was up on this gag, too. "Well," I said. "In her defense, she does have a good excuse."

"Oh, sure she does," Red said. "And what is that?"

"She passed away about five years ago."

"Shellie Charlene!" Red hollered. "You ain't right."

She is not the first one to notice.

Chicken, Herb, and Wild Rice Casserole from Kitchen Belleicious

Chicken and rice casseroles are a staple in kitchens across the South, and dinner doesn't get much easier than this over-the-top version. Rice cooked in chicken stock along with perfectly seasoned chicken, sautéed vegetables, and an abundance of herbs all work together to create the most delectable dish. The secret ingredient is ricotta cheese.

CHICKEN:

4 large frozen chicken breasts, thawed

1 teaspoon each salt and pepper

1 teaspoon thyme

1 teaspoon paprika

CASSEROLE:

1 cup white rice and 1 cup wild rice

2 cups water

2 cups chicken stock

Dash salt

1 stick unsalted butter

1 small onion, diced

1 tablespoon minced garlic

½ cup flour

½ cup milk

1 cup chicken stock

1 teaspoon Dijon mustard

¼ cup sour cream

¼ cup ricotta cheese

¾ teaspoon thyme

¾ teaspoon oregano

¼ teaspoon red pepper flakes

½ teaspoon dill

¾ teaspoon each basil and parsley

1 teaspoon chopped sage

½ cup parmesan cheese

Season chicken breasts on all sides and place on baking sheet. Bake at 400 degrees for 45 minutes until cooked through. When cool, chop into small cubes to make about 2 to 3 cups' worth.

Cook rice in 2 cups water and 2 cups chicken stock with salt added. Set aside.

Meanwhile, melt butter in large saucepan over medium to low heat. Add in chopped onion and garlic. Sauté until onions are translucent. Mix in flour; it will clump together. Reduce heat and slowly pour in milk. Add chicken stock and stir. It will be thick. Turn heat to low and add remaining ingredients except for parmesan cheese.

Combine rice and chicken in sauce. Pour into 9x13 casserole dish sprayed with cooking spray and top with parmesan cheese. Bake at 350 degrees for 30 minutes until top is slightly brown.

Fiery Sausage and Crawfish Spread

If you're a sausage fan who loves crawfish, you are sitting pretty with this one! My Fiery Sausage and Crawfish Spread is a winner at my house, and I'm betting your family will be delighted with it, too. I've also used this as a party dip, but I'm putting it in the casserole section because it can be layered on bread, rice, or pasta for a hearty one-dish meal.

½ (10 ounce) bag frozen diced green peppers, celery, and onions

1 pound hot pork sausage

Basic White Sauce (see p. 142)

4 ounces feta or a 1 pound box of Velveeta

1 pound crawfish, chopped

1 tablespoon minced garlic

1 teaspoon fish seasoning (Panola Blackened Fish Seasoning is best)

Dash hot sauce

2 loaves french bread

1 bunch green onions, chopped, for topping

Brown frozen bag of holy trinity (diced veggies) with hot pork sausage. Drain sausage and veggies and return to skillet.

In separate skillet prepare Basic White Sauce. Add feta and stir in crawfish, browned sausage, and sautéed veggies. (If you don't like feta, you can use Velveeta or the cheese of your choice, but I love the bite feta brings to this dish!) Season mixture with a tablespoon of minced garlic, teaspoon of a good fish seasoning, and dash of hot sauce.

Cook for 30 minutes over medium heat. Spoon this sauce over french bread, pasta, or rice and top with chopped green onions. It will be slap-your-mama good all three ways.

Belle Tip:

For those who aren't from the South, the "holy trinity of southern cooking" consists of chopped onion, bell pepper, and celery.

When I'm not with my mama, I'm still with my mama.
UNKNOWN

• •

*S*eeing as I've referred to Mama as the Queen of Us All several times here in this opening chapter, it occurs to me that perhaps I should explain that it is a term of endearment. I once had a disgruntled reader who thought I was being ugly about Mama. He missed my point by a country mile. I adore my mother, and I'm not being lippy when I call her the Queen of Us All. (I learned at an early age that lippy didn't pay with Mama. I was just a teenager the last time I gave her some lip in public, but the lesson stuck like white on rice.) Besides, y'all should know that if Mama gets enough of my little funnies, she'll let me know. Mama can take care of Mama.

What my readers who aren't from the South need to know is that we don't just put up with our matriarchs here in the South, we treasure them. Indeed, I'm training to be one myself because, to put it simply, matriarchs know things. I would say that if you don't believe it, just ask them, but that's not necessary either. Matriarchs are known for volunteering information.

Their accumulated knowledge is a good thing, too. Matriarchs use it to tend to all of us, body and soul. Why, Mama's know-how is precisely why Papa can live to tell another funny. The doctor testified that the baby aspirins she had Papa take that fateful morning when his heart started hurting actually saved his life. We have all decided that the good doctor's announcement validates Mama's vast medical expertise. The Queen has always practiced without a license, à la Granny Clampett, but we're not calling her on it. Not anymore.

True to form, Mama practiced a heap of medicine on Papa after that scary episode with his heart. That's a couple of years behind us now, so she has let his leash out somewhat, but at the time she was bound and determined that he would follow the doctor's orders during his recuperation (that would be both her advice and that of the actual medical professionals). Mama did everything for Papa. I remember him telling us kids that he didn't even have to make his mind up anymore. She was doing that for him, too!

"It's nice," Papa said, one day when he dropped by for coffee on a rare solo outing. "But it'll ruin you if you get used to it. Yesterday I went to Walmart by myself, and I had to circle the parking lot a good thirty minutes before I could get out and go inside."

"Because the lot was so full?" I asked.

Papa started grinning and his eyes disappeared. "Oh no," he said. "Because your mama wasn't there to tell me where to park!"

Crock-Pop Jambalaya

Ladling my hearty jambalaya over steaming hot rice will calm the wildest family unit. If you want to be a bona fide Cajun, you'll need to use andouille sausage for this dish, but you can stick with your family's favorite. Here's another tip: you can dice up the chicken breasts and put them straight into the slow cooker along with the other ingredients, and you can add the shrimp in the final stage without sautéing it as I recommend, but you'll get more flavor my way!

2 tablespoons butter

1 tablespoon olive oil

1 large onion, diced

1 large green pepper, diced

1 pound boneless skinless chicken breasts

½ pound package link sausage, halved and sliced into bite-size pieces

1 (28 ounce) can diced tomatoes

1 cup chicken broth

2 teaspoons dried oregano

1 teaspoon cayenne pepper

1 teaspoon poultry seasoning

1 teaspoon hot sauce

1 bay leaf

1 (16 ounce) package frozen okra

1 pound raw shrimp, peeled and deveined

2 teaspoons Cajun seasoning

2 tablespoons butter

1 tablespoon olive oil

2 cloves garlic, minced

Prepare skillet with butter and olive oil. Sauté onion and green pepper until onion is clear. Transfer to slow cooker. Sear chicken breasts in same skillet on both sides for 3 to 5 minutes. Dice into bite-size pieces.

Combine chicken, sausage, tomatoes, broth, and seasonings in slow cooker. Cook on high for 3 hours or low for 6 hours. Add okra during final hour of cooking. Sauté raw shrimp seasoned with Cajun seasoning in butter, olive oil, and garlic for 3 to 5 minutes. Transfer to slow cooker for last 15 minutes. Serve over hot rice.

Belle Tip:

You can bake your own chicken, of course, but I don't go to my supermarket without checking to see if they have fresh hot rotisserie chickens available. Even if I don't plan to use the chicken that day, I like to pull that delicious time-saving meat off and freeze it for future meals.

Easy Beef Enchiladas

My Easy Beef Enchiladas can be whipped up in a flash. They're a full meal, prepared with simple ingredients you can keep on hand for an encore.

1 medium onion, diced

1 medium green pepper, diced

1 tablespoon butter

1 pound ground beef

1 clove garlic, minced

2 (10 ounce) cans red enchilada sauce

1 (2.25 ounce) can chopped black olives

Dash Panola Hot Sauce

12 flour tortillas

8 ounces grated Monterey Jack cheese

Sauté chopped onions and peppers in tablespoon of butter. In separate skillet, brown hamburger meat and drain excess fat. Once veggies are soft and onions are clear, add garlic, enchilada sauce, and half of the black olives. Season with hot sauce, add drained beef, and let it simmer on low.

Coat large casserole dish with nonstick cooking spray and begin building enchiladas by filling twelve flour tortillas with meat sauce and grated Monterey Jack. Roll and place enchiladas side by side in your dish. Reserve a little cheese to sprinkle across top with any remaining sauce and the rest of the chopped black olives. Bake at 350 degrees until cheese melts and enchiladas are thoroughly heated.

Shellie's Mexican Lasagna

This is not your classic pasta, red sauce, and cheese version of lasagna, but I call it lasagna because of the way it's layered! Yeah, it's one of those recipes I invented from what I had on hand. I do that a lot.

1 pound ground beef, cooked and drained

2 cloves garlic, minced

1 teaspoon cumin

Dash hot sauce

12 (6 inch) corn tortillas

1 can diced green chilies

1 (2.25 ounce) can diced black olives

1 (10 ounce) can enchilada sauce

1 (15 ounce) can pinto beans

1 (10 ounce) can Ro-Tel tomatoes

8 ounces Monterey Jack cheese, grated

Fresh lettuce

Green onions, chopped

Fresh cilantro

Black pepper to taste

Season browned ground beef with minced garlic, cumin, and hot sauce. Now layer ingredients lasagna style: Place six tortillas on bottom of casserole dish sprayed with cooking spray. Across them spread half of meat, chilies, olives, enchilada sauce, pintos beans, tomatoes, and cheese. Repeat with six more tortillas and what remains of the previously halved ingredients.

Bake at 350 degrees for 40 minutes. I served this dish in squares atop a bed of lettuce and sprinkled with green onions and fresh cilantro. Have mercy! That's my Mexican Lasagna and it's good eating, from the All Things Southern kitchen to yours.

Shellie's Almost-Vegan Pizza with Mozzarella and Feta

Breathe deeply, meat lovers. The title may throw you, but you won't miss the meat, tomboy's honor. This dish was inspired by all of my family's favorite flavors. I layer them on store-bought pizza crust, top 'em with a couple of delicious cheeses, and, well, I do hate to brag, but my veggie pizza gets rave reviews. My beloved farmer even loves it, and he is a dyed-in-the-wool meat eater!

½ red onion, sliced

1 tablespoon butter

2 cups broccoli florets

Half carton cherry tomatoes

8 ounces sliced mushrooms

1 red pepper, sliced into bite-size pieces

1 orange pepper, sliced into bite-size pieces

1 yellow pepper, sliced into bite-size pieces

1 teaspoon minced garlic

2 tablespoons olive oil

1 tablespoon red wine vinegar

1 pizza crust (your choice, homemade or store-bought)

8 ounces grated mozzarella cheese

Banana pepper slices

2½ ounces feta cheese crumbles

1 teaspoon fresh basil, chopped

Salt and pepper to taste

Preheat oven to 475 degrees. Sauté red onion in butter while you prep remaining ingredients. Remove florets from broccoli, dice into bite-size pieces, and place in bowl with cherry tomatoes, sliced mushrooms, sliced peppers, and minced garlic. Yes, broccoli on pizza.

Drizzle veggies with olive oil and red wine vinegar, stir well, and spread 'em out on a cookie sheet before sliding them into the oven for 15 minutes. Meanwhile, brush olive oil over pizza crust and slide it into oven along with veggies during last 5 minutes to prebake.

When time is up, spread grated mozzarella over crust and top with broiled veggies and sautéed onion. Layer with as many banana peppers as your group would prefer and finish with feta cheese crumbles and basil. Return pizza to oven for another 6 to 8 minutes or until cheese is melted. There may not be any meat in sight, but that's okay. Once you serve it, the pizza will disappear, too!

2

MAIN COURSE MEATS

CARNIVORES ARE US

We have, as rednecks, the right to eat beef jerky.
JASE ROBERTSON OF A&E'S *DUCK DYNASTY*

$\mathcal{I}$ was having coffee with Mama and Papa when my darling mother announced, "I guess you know Uncle Rod found your daddy's teeth?" As it stood I did not know Papa had lost his teeth, and it sounded strange to hear that Uncle Rod had found them, but in my family you learn to jump in the story and go where it takes you.

And, to be clear, all of Papa's teeth weren't missing, just that partial plate he wears on the bottom. They never have fit right. Papa has a habit of taking them out every chance he gets. He also takes off his right boot whenever he sits down. He had a surgery on the nerve in his big toe that has proven as unsuccessful as that partial. Some people would make a joke here and say that Papa isn't all there even when it looks like he is, but not me. I was raised better.

"So, where were they?" I asked Mama.

"Where was what?"

"Papa's teeth!"

"Oh, in his truck, Shellie—right where he left 'em."

Mama told me that she and Papa had both checked that truck more than once, and neighbor Paula had even joined the hunt. It took Mama's little brother, Uncle Rod, returning from his road trip to make the dental discovery.

I told Papa the idea of the whole family looking for his teeth struck me as funny. I could tell it tickled him, too. Papa said he had just about decided that Lady was responsible, said she had been wearing an awfully strange grin on her face for days. At the mention of her name, Lady the Holy Ghost Dog looked up and turned her head sideways as if to say, "I ain't wearing your teeth. I got my own canines." Duly noted, Lady.

Special note, dear reader: you'll need a good set of your own choppers for this chapter. As the chapter title proudly proclaims, "Carnivores Are

Us." We routinely and heartily indulge in seafood, chicken, and beef, along with the variety of wild game our men bring in from the hunt, and we usually manage to maintain our good table manners as we are partaking in the feast. The following story is simply a notable exception I thought you might enjoy.

My middle sister, Rhonda Arlene (also known as Nana), got remarried several years ago, shortly after she had brought her fiancé, Gene, home for Christmas. Apparently, his being able to survive the experience of our extended family told her a lot about his staying power. General consensus has it that their "how we fell in love story" is a keeper, too! We've always thought Nana's cooking can make you want to slap your mama, but apparently that's not the only questionable behavior it can have on a man.

The way I understand it, Gene had previously dated a young woman who had more than a tad of trouble finding her way around the stove. The poor woman served Gene a pot roast once that almost turned that southern boy vegan. Enter my sister.

As Gene told us, he was already way past smitten with Rhonda Arlene by the time she invited him to eat pot roast at her house after church. *Oh no,* Gene thought. *I really like this woman. What am I going to do if she can't cook?* Visions of that other poisonous pot roast tormented the poor boy as the

Sunday dinner date neared.

Mind you, my sissy knew nothing of Gene's building anxiety. As she sat down to the table with her new beau, she had no idea that he considered this to be the day of reckoning. She didn't notice how tentative Gene's first forkful was, nor did she think it was that unusual when he asked for seconds and even thirds. But it was impossible for her to miss his final enthusiastic assessment. Imagine my sissy's shock when her sweetie picked up his plate and licked it whistle clean.

Licked. The. Plate. Clean.

A very embarrassed Gene says he doesn't remember the moment he lost all sense of control, but he'll never forget meeting Rhonda's incredulous look over the top of her brightly colored Fiestaware.

I say, that's the kind of compliment that cements a relationship. If the way to a man's heart is through his stomach, licking the plate has got to be his love language.

Nana's Plate-Licking Pot Roast

I have managed to secure for y'all the details of that legendary plate-licking pot roast. Seeing as it is something of a love potion, I recommend being very careful as to whose feet are under your table when it is served.

1 chuck roast

Salt and pepper to taste

1 package dry onion soup mix

1 can french onion soup

1 can golden mushroom soup

1 bag baby carrots

6 potatoes, cut into 1-inch pieces

Spray slow cooker (or dutch oven) with cooking spray. Place roast in bottom, and salt and pepper it well. Mix soups together in large bowl, refilling cans with water as you go, swirling it around to rinse insides of cans. Use this liquid, too. Pour combined soups over roast. Halfway through cooking time add carrots and potatoes.

Cook on low for 6 to 8 hours or for 4 to 5 hours at 300 degrees. The meat should fork apart without effort and catch a husband with ease.

*I am not a glutton—
I am an explorer of food.*

Erma Bombeck

New Year's Red Pepper Roast

Some people might think I'm being risky putting my Red Pepper Roast right next door to Nana's Plate-Licking Pot Roast, but they each deserve a place in your repertoire. This one also makes delicious sliders, sliced and served with my Peppered Butter on sweet Hawaiian rolls. Yum!

ROAST:

1 (4 to 5 pound) beef roast

⅓ cup Dijon mustard

4 tablespoons coarsely ground mixed peppercorns

PEPPERED BUTTER:

6 tablespoons softened butter

¼ cup bottled roasted red peppers, drained and finely chopped (find my instructions for roasting your own peppers on page 181)

1½ tablespoons dried basil

1½ tablespoons dried parsley

Rub beef roast with Dijon mustard. Sprinkle liberally with ground peppercorns and place on raised rack in shallow roasting pan. Roast at 350 degrees until thickest section registers at least 150 degrees on meat thermometer (1 to 1½ hours, depending on size of roast).

Meanwhile, prepare Peppered Butter by beating butter until fluffy and adding roasted red peppers, basil, and parsley. (Fresh herbs are even better if you have them on hand!)

That's it! Serve roast as main dish and use butter for your meal's bread or slice meat thin and serve on rolls with peppered butter for party sandwiches. It's a winner either way.

Throw-Back Chicken Fried Steak

Despite the stereotype, most of the southern cooks in my circle have quit eating a lot of fried foods, with a few notable exceptions. Old-fashioned chicken fried steak is one of those time-honored southern dishes we feel is worthy of exception, so don't be looking for us to let go of it anytime soon. Oh, and do serve this with mashed potatoes or it's almost a crime.

STEAK:

1 cup flour

Salt and pepper to taste

2 pounds round steak cut into serving sizes and beaten thin with kitchen mallet

1 egg, beaten

¼ cup butter

GRAVY:

3 tablespoons flour

3 tablespoons fat (pan drippings after frying steak)

2 cups cold water

Salt and pepper to taste

Season flour with salt and pepper; flour steaks well. Dip in beaten egg and dredge in flour again. Heat butter, add steaks, and cook over medium heat 3 to 4 minutes per side. Don't overcook! Move steaks to warm oven and prepare gravy.

Add 3 tablespoons flour to pan drippings. (If you don't have quite enough drippings, add a little more butter.) Stir flour until brown, and pour in water. Continue to stir while bringing to a boil. Reduce heat and cook 5 to 10 minutes. Season with salt and pepper to taste and serve with steaks.

The Belle's Reimagined Meat Loaf

Meat loaf has never been a favorite of mine or the farmer's. I think he had a few too many back in the day. However, I took meat loaf over the top with some new ingredients, and my sauce plays a big hand in it.

MEAT:

1½ pounds ground beef

2 cups crushed saltine crackers

1 cup milk

1 egg

1 white onion, diced

2 tablespoons butter

1 tablespoon crushed red pepper flakes

2 teaspoons minced garlic

1 teaspoon Tony Chachere's Original Creole Seasoning

Black pepper

SAUCE:

1 cup ketchup

1 capful balsamic vinegar

2 tablespoons brown sugar

½ teaspoon dry mustard

Mix uncooked ground beef with crackers, milk, and egg. Sauté diced white onion in butter and add to beef. (No more raw onions going into my meat loaf. Caramelize those babies, and they'll add a lot more flavor.) Season meat mixture with red pepper flakes, minced garlic, creole seasoning, and pepper. Instead of making one large loaf, I like to form mine into nice-sized servings—like you would with hamburger steaks.

Prepare sauce by combining all ingredients in small bowl. Place loaves on raised grill in roasting pan (to catch drippings) and pour sauce across them. Bake uncovered at 350 degrees for 1 hour 15 minutes.

Strapping Burgers

Fire up the grill and put on a bunch of my Strapping Burgers,
but be warned: there's nothing timid about these babies.
You'll want to check your diet at the screen door!

2 pounds ground beef

Salt and pepper to taste

2 tablespoons dried parsley

1 teaspoon garlic powder

1 tablespoon soy sauce

1 tablespoon steak sauce

Dash hot sauce

8 to 10 slices bacon, fried and crumbled

2 (2.5 ounce) jars mushroom pieces

1½ cups grated Monterey Jack cheese

Season ground beef with salt and pepper and mix in parsley, garlic powder, soy sauce, steak sauce, and dash of My All Things Southern Comeback Sauce (see page 145 for recipe) or another hot sauce. Pat seasoned meat into 16 very thin patties. Top 8 patties with bacon, mushroom pieces, and Monterey Jack. Place a second thin patty on top of each of these and press edges together to seal.

Throw 'em on a hot grill until they're at the readiness you enjoy. Have mercy, that's good eating, southern style!

Belle Tip:

If possible, avoid the cheese shreds in the bag. Save money and gain flavor by grating your own cheese.

A voice came to him, "Get up, Peter, kill and eat!"
ACTS 10:13 NASB

⬩──⬩

Despite the aforementioned pot roast incident, as a general rule my people do not believe that eating meat leads to questionable behavior. We're at peace with the whole food chain idea and the good Lord's admonition to "get up, kill and eat."

Mind you, I wouldn't even feel the need to stake out our position in these pages were it not for the most bizarre study that was recently released by one of our country's esteemed universities. To protect yours truly from potential litigation, I won't be identifying this particular institute of higher learning, but I will recap their findings.

A number of otherwise highly intelligent people claim to have discovered a strong connection between eating meat and overly aggressive personalities. After conducting serious research—at a summer camp for kids—the behavioral scientists concluded that biting into food with their front teeth could be bringing out our children's natural aggression.

If I understood correctly, it's still okay for Junior to chew his food. The danger stems more from chomping down on a chicken leg and tearing off a bite. They recommend lowering the stress level by cutting the family's food into bite-size pieces before sitting down to dine together. That, and seeing that everyone eats with utensils. The silverware detail is important because, according to the report, seeing other loved ones baring their front teeth could leave Junior "feeling threatened and thereby escalate his own violent behavior."

Are y'all still with me?

I think studies like this are best used to remind us that book sense can be overrated. It's good old common sense that will keep you out of trouble. For illustration, I give you the following story from a Louisiana belle currently living in the fine Show-Me State of Missouri.

Christy was having lunch by herself in her favorite barbecue joint when she noticed a man at a nearby table staring directly at her. The stranger had crazy-big eyes, and he was licking his lips and smacking loudly. Taken together, the man's appearance and the way he was acting gave Christy the creeps and convinced her that he was liable to be a serial killer. (Granted, he could've simply encountered a tough piece of meat, but belles are nothing if not dramatic.)

Seriously freaked out by the whole thing, Christy did what she had to do. As the stranger watched, Christy bit into her sandwich and chewed around on a big piece of barbecue before spitting the mouthful back out onto her plate slowly, very slowly. It worked. The possible serial killer exited quickly: stage left.

Christy said her daddy had always told her that in the face of stranger danger, she should act crazier than the madman. Note to the intellectual community: now, that's what I call thinking outside the box.

Oven-Baked Ribs That Won't Ever Miss the Grill

The weather doesn't always cooperate when you're in the mood for barbecued ribs. Keep this recipe handy, and you can enjoy all of that flavor whenever you'd like, indoors!

MEAT:

2 Vidalia onions

4 pounds pork ribs

1 tablespoon vegetable oil

SAUCE:

1 cup ketchup

1 cup balsamic vinegar ketchup

2 cups water

1 teaspoon salt

¼ cup Worcestershire sauce

½ cup white vinegar

¾ cup light brown sugar

4 teaspoons dry mustard

2 cloves garlic, crushed

Preheat oven to 350 degrees. Slice Vidalia onions and set aside. With knife, split ribs between bones, making portions 3 to 4 ribs each. Rinse and drain on paper towels. Sear on both sides in cast-iron skillet coated with vegetable oil. This will give ribs a pretty crust instead of that pasty meat look an oven tends to produce.

While ribs are searing, prepare sauce by combining ketchups with remaining ingredients. Place seared ribs in single layer in large baking dish and pour half of the sauce over them. Reserve remaining sauce. Bake ribs for 3 hours, basting heavily every 30 to 40 minutes until sauce is gone. Enjoy!

Bacon-Wrapped Pork Chops with Balsamic and Brown Sugar Glaze

Have y'all seen the wafer-thin pork chops in your local grocery? If not, you really need to look for them. They're the star of this dish. Lights, camera, action!

PORK CHOPS:

5 very thin pork chops

10 slices peppered bacon

GLAZE:

1½ cups light brown sugar

2 tablespoons flour

2 teaspoons spicy brown mustard

3 tablespoons balsamic vinegar

Wrap individual pork chops in 2 strips peppered bacon. Place on broiler pan and bake at 350 degrees for 15 minutes. Flip chops and return to oven 15 minutes more.

While pork chops are baking, prepare glaze in small saucepan. Mix all ingredients, heat to boiling, then reduce heat and simmer 1 to 2 minutes. Once sauce thickens, remove from heat.

When pork chops have baked 15 minutes on each side, brush one side with sauce and place under broiler 3 to 4 minutes. When bacon begins to crisp, turn chops, baste again, and return to broiler until second side is crispy.

The meat lovers at your table will love these bacon-wrapped pork chops.

Barbecue Pork Chops

When I was a little girl, an older boy on our school bus harassed me by telling me I was so ugly my parents had to tie a pork chop around my neck to get the dogs to play with me. I knew it was an insult, but for the life of me, I thought the visual was funny. This was not the reaction he expected. My Barbecue Pork Chops are reminiscent of my oven-baked ribs, and they'll exceed expectations, too, in the best possible way. Serve the two together if you're feeding a crowd.

6 center-cut pork chops, fat trimmed

1 tablespoon vegetable oil

1 (14.5 ounce) can crushed tomatoes

½ cup ketchup

¼ cup dark brown sugar

3 tablespoons Worcestershire sauce

2 tablespoons prepared mustard

Dash hot sauce

Salt and pepper to taste

Preheat oven to 350 degrees. Brown chops on both sides in vegetable oil.

Meanwhile, in mixing bowl, combine tomatoes, ketchup, and brown sugar. Season with Worcestershire sauce, mustard, and hot sauce. Add salt and pepper to taste. Stir well.

Layer in 9x13 baking dish. Spoon sauce over top and bake for 45 minutes.

Those bones are going to be whistle clean.

Belle Tip:

Make sure you buy nice big bone-in pork chops. You'll get more flavor from the bone.

Hangry (han-gree) adj.: a state of
anger caused by lack of food.

My spoiled-rotten chocolate Lab knows my schedule inside and out, and she's always one step ahead of me. If I leave by the front door after my early morning devotion, Dixie Belle knows I'm going for a walk. Should I exit through the back porch headed toward the lake, Dixie knows it's kayak time. This is the old girl's clue to start fretting. Because Dixie takes her security detail seriously, she feels compelled to position herself on the dock during my kayak time and bark without pause, all to ensure my safety. She begins barking when I leave, and she's still barking when I return. My apologies to our neighbors. I've tried to break her of it, but the crazy canine is hopelessly neurotic about me being on the water.

Indeed, Dixie and I are such creatures of habit that even the bird population around here has begun setting their clocks by our routine. It's my custom to toss a couple of doggie bones in the backyard for Dixie when I first arrive on the back porch for my morning devotion. It is Dixie's custom to have them devoured before I can get past "Dear Lord." Three circles and one belly flop later, she settles into her favorite spot in the shade—one step ahead of the birds. They've learned that Dixie's enthusiastic eating style always leaves crumbs for the next hungry group on the food chain.

I was watching the birds feasting on Dixie's leftovers one morning when I began to think of how that small glimpse of the food chain reminds me of the great value of giving ourselves to the study of God's Word, not only for our own growth, but for the nourishment of those around us. While it can be difficult to articulate what we're learning from the scriptures, there is multiplied benefit in the practice. It's only when we tax ourselves to chew on a passage of God's Word until we're able to express the treasure we've found in it, that the life-sustaining truth we're enjoying can become broken down bread to share with others.

Granted, the ideal situation would be for the next group to digest it and pass it on, too. But I think the big question for you and me would be: Where are we on this holy food chain?

You could talk to him as well as you could to many
human beings, and better than you could to some.
WILLIE MORRIS, *MY DOG SKIP*

TANGIPAHOA SHRIMP FROM KITCHEN BELLEICIOUS

One of my husband's favorite dishes is barbecued shrimp, or as he calls it, Tangipahoa Shrimp. He's from New Orleans, where this dish reigns, but you'd be hard-pressed to find anyone from the Deep South who doesn't love this ridiculously savory and rich dish.

3 pounds large Gulf shrimp, in shells

1½ teaspoons each salt and pepper

1 stick butter

1 small onion, diced

3 cloves garlic, minced

3 bay leaves

3 tablespoons thyme

3 tablespoons basil

3 tablespoons parsley

1 tablespoon oregano

1 tablespoon Cajun seasoning

Dash hot sauce

1 lemon, juiced

12 ounces dark beer

½ cup Worcestershire sauce

3 green onions, chopped

Season shrimp generously with salt and pepper and spread out evenly in skillet, casserole dish, or your choice of pan (as long as it has at least 2 inches depth). Set aside.

Melt butter in medium saucepan and add onions and garlic. Sauté until tender, 5 to 6 minutes. Add herbs, seasoning, and hot sauce. Slowly pour in lemon juice, beer, and Worcestershire sauce and bring to simmer. Simmer covered for 10 to 20 minutes (the longer, the better the flavor). Stir in green onions and pour mixture over shrimp. Bake at 350 degrees for 15 to 20 minutes.

Pulled Mexican Lime Chicken from Kitchen Belleicious

One day I found myself in the mood to do something different with pulled chicken. We eat a ton of barbecue, so I decided to use Mexican flavors alongside the classic sauce staples and then pair it with tacos. The flavors of lime, jalapeño, and green chilies are strong yet not too overpowering, and the vinegar, sugar, and ketchup bring a sweetness to the chicken that creates a wonderful combination of sweet and heat.

4 chicken breasts

Salt and pepper to season

¾ cup ketchup

½ cup water

2 tablespoons apple cider vinegar

2 tablespoons jalapeño juice

1 large lime, juiced, plus 2 limes cut for the slow cooker

⅛ cup brown sugar

1 small can green chilies, drained

½ cup salsa

1 small onion, diced

1½ tablespoons chopped cilantro (more for garnish if you'd like)

2 cloves garlic, minced

1 teaspoon each salt and pepper

1 teaspoon cumin

½ teaspoon paprika

½ teaspoon chili powder

Place chicken breasts in slow cooker and season well with salt and pepper. In medium mixing bowl, stir together ketchup, water, apple cider vinegar, jalapeño juice, and juice of a large lime. Add brown sugar, drained green chilies, and salsa (use your favorite).

Add diced onion to sauce with chopped cilantro, minced garlic, salt, pepper, cumin, paprika, and chili powder.

Pour sauce over chicken breasts and place lime slices around them. Cover the slow cooker and cook on low for 5½ hours. To serve, transfer chicken breasts to large bowl and pull apart before spooning ½ cup of slow-cooker juice over pulled meat and gently stirring it to coat. You're done! Discard limes and serve chicken on your favorite buns, taco shells, or tortillas.

Spicy Chicken Drummettes

The dressing mix ramps up the flavor of these drummettes; the vinegar and hot sauce deliver the spice. Take these to a big get-together or serve them for your own family's enjoyment. Either way, you'll make them again and again.

3 tablespoons vinegar

½ cup melted butter

¼ cup hot sauce

24 chicken drummettes

1 package Hidden Valley Ranch Original dry salad dressing mix

Prepare sauce in small bowl by stirring together vinegar, melted butter, and hot sauce. Place drummettes in slow cooker and pour sauce over top. Sprinkle with dry dressing mix and cook on low for 4 to 5 hours. Enjoy!

Belle Tip:

Sometimes I sear these before placing them in the slow cooker to get a prettier color, but I've noticed they disappear either way!

BUTTERMILK CHICKEN

Perhaps you're not a fan of buttermilk as a drink. Nor am I. In my opinion, buttermilk is for cooking, period. I still haven't totally forgiven my papa for switching my whole milk for buttermilk while my eyes were closed during the blessing—and that's been years ago! But, I promise, you won't know this delicious chicken dish is cooked in buttermilk. It'll be our secret.

1 clove garlic, crushed

2 cups buttermilk, divided

2 tablespoons Worcestershire sauce

¼ teaspoon sea salt

Dash Worchestershire sauce

Dash My All Things Southern Comeback Sauce (see p. 145)

6 to 8 chicken breasts

1 cup flour seasoned with salt and pepper

Olive oil for browning

1 can cream of mushroom soup

½ cup chopped green onion

½ cup sour cream

Prepare marinade by combining crushed garlic with 1 cup buttermilk, Worcestershire sauce, sea salt, and hot sauce in plastic bag. Use it to marinate chicken breasts for 2 to 3 hours. Remove breasts, coat with flour, then brown in olive oil in hot skillet.

Once breasts are golden brown on both sides, remove from skillet and place in baking dish. In small bowl, stir together remaining buttermilk, cream of mushroom soup, green onion, Worcestershire sauce, and sour cream. Spread over chicken breasts and bake in 350-degree oven for another 30 minutes or until breasts are no longer pink and juices run clear.

BLACK OLIVE AND SALSA CHICKEN

Choose the level of heat your family enjoys with the salsa of your choice, or experiment with the multitude of salsas on the market. But do keep chicken breasts in the freezer and your pantry stocked with the rest of the ingredients for my Black Olive and Salsa Chicken, and you will always have supplies on hand for a tasty meal.

4 boneless, skinless chicken breasts

½ teaspoon finely chopped garlic

1 (16 ounce) jar chunky salsa

1 (2.25 ounce) can sliced black olives, drained

Beat chicken breasts to uniform thickness. Spray nonstick frying pan with olive oil cooking spray. Sauté garlic over low heat. Add chicken and cook over low to medium heat until golden, turning once. Add salsa and cover. Cook over medium-low heat 30 to 40 minutes. Serve over rice and top with sliced black olives.

You don't need a silver fork to eat good food.

PAUL PRUDHOMME

$\mathcal{B}$less my loved ones' collective hearts. They live in a state of heightened awareness on my behalf, seeing as how I talk for a living and, for the most part, I do not have a working filter. My family realizes that it's becoming increasingly hard to speak in the public square without offending someone somewhere.

Pardon me for going all eighth grade, but whatever. The PC police remind me of the hall monitors in elementary school who had an overinflated opinion of their importance. They're always trying to strike yet another word or phrase from our vocabulary because they've now deemed it offensive. While I admit some words might need to fall out of favor, I would also humbly like to suggest that anyone who is bound and determined to be offended will be.

For instance, if I had a mind to, I could be offended on behalf of catfish. That's right. Catfish.

I know about catfish. I know how to hold them so they won't cut you with their fins, I know the sound of their "voice," and I know how to batter and fry them regardless of how much they try and talk you out of it. What I did not know until recently is that there are people who define a catfish as "someone who creates a false identity online, particularly to pursue deceptive online romances."

And herein lies my point. Of all people, we southerners are the most closely identified with catfish, but you've heard nary a word of protest from us over the word being used in a derogatory manner, now have you? Of course not. We aren't going to riot because you've vilified our catfish. We're not going to hold sit-ins or sit-outs. We're just going to sit down to another mess of fillets and hush puppies and laugh at y'all. I mean, let it go. That's right, we're just going to let it go.

Whew. That was close.

Changing the subject. . .I was kayaking down the lake awhile back minding my own business when I saw a water bottle ahead of me, bobbing up and down in the water. Seconds later it disappeared, only to pop right back up and start swimming! You heard right. The water bottle began swimming around all crazy-like as it continued to sink and resurface, sink and resurface! I realized something had ahold of it because I'm smart like that. My inquiring mind had to know what that something was.

I drew alongside the bobbing water bottle and steeled my nerves by assuring myself that whatever was jerking it around couldn't be that big—and then I picked the bottle up, slowly. Whoa! To my surprise, I found a nice-sized catfish dangling from a short fishing line, hooked firmly in its poor bottom lip. Someone had tied the other end of the two foot line around the mouth of the bottle and twisted the top back on for good measure.

Now, I've eaten my share of fried catfish, but I'll be honest: this cat's plight made me sad even before he commenced telling me his side of the story. Yes, catfish do talk, and this one was mighty wound up! I'm not fluent in catfish chat, but I decided he was telling me that some cruel teenager had rigged him up to spend his dying fish days fighting that water bottle, which is why I sorta, kinda—well, here's the thing: I released him. And that's why I feel compelled to air this open apology.

> Dear Mr. Fisherman,
>
> Should you ever run across this little tale of mine, there is something I want you to know. Once the men in my family finally quit laughing at this story, they told me I had happened upon a low-tech form of yo-yo fishing. Uh-oh. Sir, I'm familiar with trotlines and yo-yos—but seriously, it never occurred to me that you were fishing with that water bottle rig or that you would be coming back to check it.
>
> My bad.
>
> The guys had a big time imagining you watching from somewhere nearby as I took selfies with your supper and released it back into the lake. They imagined you possibly muttering under your breath, "She can't be doing what I think she's doing."
>
> They also assure me that I had been in no danger pulling up that bottle, at least not from the fish. Again, I'm sorry, Mr. Fisherman. But hey, look on the bright side. You've got yourself a really good story about the one that got away.

Shellie's Mind-Changing Fish Tacos

My man has never found the words fish tacos *all that appetizing. He's a "Where's the beef?" type of guy when it comes to tacos. That said, I've made a believer out of Phil, and I'm confident I can make a believer out of you, too.*

4 to 6 tilapia fillets

1 teaspoon Cajun seasoning

2 to 3 tablespoons balsamic vinegar

2 to 3 tablespoons Worcestershire sauce

2 to 3 tablespoons olive oil

Juice of 1 lemon

Tomatoes, diced

Green onions, diced

Lettuce, shredded

Guacamole

Flour tortillas

Vegetable oil for frying

Grated Monterey Jack cheese

Salsa

Fresh cilantro

Season fillets with Cajun seasoning and sear on both sides in hot cast-iron skillet. Stir together balsamic vinegar, Worcestershire sauce, and olive oil, then pour over seared fillets and turn heat down to medium. Cook 8 to 12 minutes, depending on thickness of fillets. Tilapia is ready when it flakes easily with fork and reveals pretty white flesh. Sprinkle cooked fish with lemon juice and let it rest.

Meanwhile, dice tomatoes and green onions, shred lettuce, and prepare fresh guacamole. (You can find my guacamole recipe on page 141.)

Now, here's what took 'em over the top for us. Sometimes nothing takes the place of frying, and this is one of those times for me. Fry fresh tortillas in an inch of hot vegetable oil for 1 to 2 minutes. Remove tortillas when you can still fold them without them cracking in two.

Drain tortillas on paper towels. Stuff with forked fish and veggies. Top with Monterey Jack, guacamole, salsa, and cilantro. Prepare enough for your family to have seconds. They'll be back for more!

Honey Butter Glazed Salmon from Kitchen Belleicious

Some people think salmon is difficult to cook. It's not. Here's a marinade and technique that will deliver big flavor without that "fishy" taste that can give it a bad rap.

4 tablespoons honey

4 tablespoons olive oil, divided

5 tablespoons butter, melted

3 tablespoons soy sauce

1½ tablespoons minced garlic

2 teaspoons black sesame seeds

1 teaspoon salt

1 teaspoon cracked black pepper

4 salmon fillets or 1 large (1.5 pound) fillet, with skin

Combine all ingredients except salmon. Place salmon in large ziplock bag or pan and season with dashes of salt and pepper. Remove and drizzle with marinade mixture—just enough to coat salmon. You should have at least ¼ to ⅓ cup left. Reserve remaining marinade.

Heat nonstick skillet over high heat. Drizzle with 1 tablespoon olive oil. Place salmon skin-side down and cook for 3 to 4 minutes. Spoon just enough marinade over salmon to coat, then flip salmon over so skin is faceup. Turn heat to medium-low and cook for another 4 to 5 minutes while you continue to baste fillets in remaining marinade (I spoon mixture over top and sides). As you spoon marinade over salmon, it will fall down into pan and begin to thicken at sides and edges of fillets. Cook until salmon is flaky and slightly pulling apart (approximately 4 to 5 minutes). Serve immediately.

Shellie's Pork Tenderloin Perfected

*Over the years, I've cooked pork tenderloin in a dozen different ways.
I still have a handful of flavor favorites, but this is the only one I call Pork
Tenderloin Perfected because it delivers moist, tender pork every single time.
Play around with different seasonings and sauces if you like,
but stick to the steps for a fail-proof entrée.*

PORK:

1 (3 pound) pork tenderloin

Salt and pepper to taste

Cajun seasoning

Crushed peppercorns

SAUCE:

2 tablespoons molasses

2 tablespoons soy sauce

2 tablespoons brown sugar

1 teaspoon ginger

1 teaspoon crushed garlic

1 teaspoon balsamic vinegar

Preheat oven to 550 degrees. Calculate cooking time based on tenderloin size. For every pound, cook it 5½ minutes—no more, no less. (That means you'll cook this 3-pound tenderloin 16½ minutes.)

Prepare tenderloin by rubbing it down with your favorite seasonings. I use salt, pepper, and a good Cajun seasoning along with some crushed peppercorns. Place rubbed tenderloin in roasting pan, uncovered, and put it in oven. When cooking time expires, turn oven off but do not open door for a full hour. That's the trick that will keep it cooking to perfection. After an hour, remove tenderloin and allow it to rest 5 to 10 minutes before slicing. Simple yet delicious.

For sauce, combine all ingredients and thicken on stovetop. Pour over resting tenderloin. You could also use this sauce for a marinade if you'd like, but either way, it's good eating.

Belle Tip:

Remember to allow the meat to rest before slicing it. The meat will absorb and retain more of its natural juices.

SWEET AND SAUCY PORK LOIN

This is another of my pork tenderloin recipes. Use this one when you can't watch the meat as closely as you need to in Pork Tenderloin Perfected. Six simple ingredients and three steps for a melt-in-your-mouth tasty pork tenderloin. Let me walk you through it.

1 tablespoon Cajun seasoning

1 teaspoon pepper

1 teaspoon garlic powder

1 small (2 to 3 pound) pork tenderloin

½ pound peppered bacon

1 small jar apricot preserves

First, stir together Cajun seasoning, pepper, and garlic powder, then rub well into pork loin.

Next, wrap individual slices of peppered bacon around pork loin and place in cast-iron skillet.

Finally, spoon apricot preserves over tenderloin and cook uncovered for 45 to 60 minutes at 350 degrees or until meat thermometer reads 150 degrees. (The temperature will rise another ten degrees or so while it rests.) Briefly broil tenderloin if you prefer a crunchier bacon finish. I do.

Make a sauce by deglazing skillet with a bit of chicken broth, wine, or liquid of your choice. Yum!

BELLE TIP:
You can also cook tenderloin on low in your slow cooker until the meat shreds easily with a fork.

Company Ham

*My son would be happy if every holiday came with a baked ham,
but he is certain that Christmas isn't complete without one.
This is the ham I serve, and it always gets rave reviews.*

1 (12 to 13 pound) ham
3½ cups brown sugar
⅓ cup balsamic vinegar
1 teaspoon dry mustard
½ teaspoon ground cloves

Place ham cut side down in cast-iron skillet. Tent with foil and place in 325-degree oven for 10 minutes per pound. Uncooked ham will require 20 minutes per pound. Uncooked ham must bake until it reaches an internal temperature of 160 degrees.

To make glaze, blend brown sugar with vinegar and season with dry mustard and ground cloves. Remove ham from oven 20 minutes before end of total cooking time. Score with diamond pattern and coat with glaze. Stud with whole cloves if desired. Return ham to oven for 20 minutes.

Remove from oven and let stand at least 30 minutes before slicing to retain juices.

Be hospitable to one another without complaint.
1 Peter 4:9 NASB

$\mathcal{W}$e did the neatest thing last Christmas. It's something I wished I would've done with some of our other relatives who are no longer with us, but live and learn, that's my motto.

As my daughter-in-law and I began clearing the gumbo dishes one evening, my husband and our son started asking my father-in-law questions designed to get him into storytelling mode. For the record, getting Grandbuzzy to tell stories is about as difficult as getting a sermon from a Baptist preacher.

Like so many southerners, Grandbuzzy is a natural-born storyteller. He had already warmed up his audience by the time I returned and started setting up my video cam to capture the show! He watched me with great interest, but he didn't pause in his current tale, at least not until I began pinning a small microphone to the greenery on the table's centerpiece.

"And who are you with?" Grandbuzzy asked. "The NSA?"

I assured my father-in-law that I wasn't with the federal government, and he could continue, not that he really needed much prompting. Once Grandbuzzy primes the pump, stories flow effortlessly. It does my heart good to know that we now have a good many of them recorded for his descendants.

One of my personal favorites was Grandbuzzy telling about the time he and a couple of friends were flying around in his small plane scouting for deer. Do note they weren't going to shoot them out of the plane—that's illegal. This was more about looking for signs and promising trails.

During their flight, however, they noticed a small pond full of ducks. Well, now, seeing as it was duck season, too, the hunters swapped targets faster than quick. They landed that plane a good ways off and began making their way toward the ducks, quietly and stealthily.

Once they snuck up close enough, they dropped down and belly crawled the last hundred or so yards until they were positioned just at the water's edge. Grandbuzzy said he and his friends had gotten their feet under them in the brush and were about to stand up and fire away when they heard a lone voice say, "Hey, y'all aren't gonna shoot my decoys—are you?"

When an old man dies, a library burns to the ground.
OLD AFRICAN PROVERB

Dirty Rice with Duck

We love waterfowl season here in Louisiana. Roast duck, duck gumbo, grilled duck, fried duck—the men at my house are responsible for killin' and cleanin' 'em; I'm the cook. Let me show y'all how to whip up my dirty rice recipe.

2 large duck breasts

1 tablespoon olive oil

1 pound bulk pork sausage

1 large white onion, chopped

1 bunch green onions, chopped

1 bell pepper, chopped

2 stalks celery, chopped

1 garlic clove, chopped

2 cups uncooked rice

Salt and pepper to taste

Dash Panola hot sauce

2 tablespoons Worcestershire sauce

1 teaspoon Cajun seasoning

1 (15 ounce) can chicken broth

3½ cups water

Slice duck breasts into sizes that will fit in your food processor. Rinse and drain on paper towels and spin in food processor to chop meat up even more. Brown in olive oil.

Partially brown pork sausage. Add partially ground duck and cook together over medium heat for 10 to 15 minutes to let flavors mingle.

Remove meat, reserving drippings to sauté onion, pepper, celery, and garlic in. Once veggies are tender, put them in large soup pot with meat and rice. Season well with salt and pepper, hot sauce, Worcestershire sauce, and Cajun seasoning. Add chicken broth and water. Bring to boil on stove, reduce heat, cover, and cook on low another 30 minutes or until rice is done and liquid is absorbed.

3

My Favorite Go-To Breads

ROAD TRIPPING WITH THE BELLE

If I'm performing in a country fair in upstate New York and I say, "Me and Marcel went coon huntin'"... I explain coon huntin'. If I'm in Alabama, I just say, "We went coon hunting," and go right on with the story.

JERRY CLOWER

*M*ama has issues with me traveling alone to my speaking engagements. I need to check in on a regular basis to keep her from standing on her own head worrying about whether someone has knocked me in the back of mine. Being knocked in the back of the head may sound like a random act of violence, but if Mama's level of concern is any indication, people get knocked in the back of the head more often than any of us realize. Apparently, you don't have to worry about people knocking you in the front of the head. They're sneakier than that. But they will knock you in the back of the head in a New York minute.

If I'm not talking to my husband as I make my way from parking lot to hotel room, Mama likes me to be on the phone with her, you know, to thwart any such underhanded attacks on my head.

I've never exactly figured out how it's going to help if I'm on the phone with her, unless the knocker person is already feeling guilty or is close to his own mama. If that's the case, I suppose I could say, "Would you please? I'm talking to Mama!" In theory, this is the point at which he would apologize scurry off with his tail tucked between his legs. (I've heard about that body posture all my life. It sounds like quite the contortionist trick to me, but I try not to think about it because it's difficult to erase the mental image.)

Fortunately for me, Mama is always alerting me to all possible head-knocking scenarios. For instance, it worries her to no end when I'm flying to a speaking engagement where the plan is for me to be picked up and taken to my hotel by a stranger holding a sign with my name on it. Mama is concerned that it's a trap and no one will ever hear from me again.

"What exactly are you saying?" I asked Mama not long back. "That someone would go to the trouble of finding where I'm headed next and what flight I'm going to be on, all to make a fake sign and kidnap me?"

Mama raised her eyebrows. "That's exactly what I'm saying, Shellie Charlene. Stranger things have happened."

She had me there.

I say this with great love and affection for my Georgia readers, but I wouldn't be the least surprised if the majority of those strange things happened in Atlanta. I once made a big honking announcement that I would never connect in Atlanta again, so help me Scarlett O'Hara. I didn't blame my readers for laughing. It was only a matter of time before I had to eat those words. As they say, "You can't get anywhere without going through Atlanta."

On the bright side, however, I used my last visit there to further develop a theory I've been working on about Atlanta International. Here's the short of it—I believe the employees suffer from an extreme form of claustrophobia that has led them to create a top-secret inside game. Think scavenger hunt. The last-minute gate changes we abhor are orchestrated to help them fill out their score cards.

Points are awarded for documenting crying babies, fighting couples, and out-of-breath grandmothers trying to fake injuries to get onto one of those special needs trains, which I now agree is flat-out wrong.

I'm pretty sure the sweet young thang staffing the check-in counter at D33 got bonus points off of my last terminal run. I arrived at her desk with a second to spare and breathed out what I hoped sounded like a cheery sort of moan. She knew the signs.

"Where'd you come from?" she asked.

"A21," I said between great gulps of air. "Check your screen."

Her eyes widened as she noted my arrival time, calculated the distance between the two terminals at opposite ends of the world, and computed my record-setting feat: 5.3 minutes! I appreciated her high five, and the picture we took in celebration is a nice memento, but still.

If you aren't playing Run That Terminal in Atlanta, it's usually because you've been drawn into another of their favorite games: Delay Purgatory. Yes, it is true. A plane leaves the Atlanta airport every thirty seconds, but when you're in Delay Purgatory, none of them will be yours, silly. But don't get comfortable, or at least make sure you don't appear to be at rest. Should an airport employee notice that you've pulled out your reading or work materials and set up your home away from home at one gate, they'll switch you to another gate in a faraway time zone faster than you can say, "Hey, I forgot my Cinnabon!"

Fortunately, Atlanta International has compensated for the distance between terminals with supersonic trams that run between concourses at the speed of light. FYI: when the nice intercom lady reminds you to brace yourself because the train is now departing the station, I would not consider that a mere suggestion unless you want to do the mosh pit thing into a sea of equally disgruntled travelers.

Not that I've ever done that.

Tomato Onion Tart with Cornmeal Crust from Kitchen Belleicious

Can you say "savory" ten times in a row while balancing a spoon on your nose, holding a glass of water, and jumping up and down? No? I didn't think so. Instead, let's make it simple and just stand there and scream, "This is the best dang tomato tart I have ever had, hands down!" Now, that was easier, wasn't it? This appetizer is easier than it looks. Make the dough, let it rest, and prebake the crust before drowning it with the yummy tomatoes and onions.

1½ tablespoons olive oil

1 large onion, thinly sliced

2 cloves garlic, minced

1½ teaspoons balsamic vinegar, divided

½ teaspoon each salt and pepper

Dash paprika

1 teaspoon sugar

2 large ripe tomatoes, thinly sliced

½ cup shredded mozzarella cheese

½ cup shredded parmesan cheese

2 tablespoons chopped basil or parsley

Olive oil for drizzling

Dash each kosher salt and pepper

CRUST:

1 package active yeast

1 cup warm water

½ teaspoon sugar

1½ teaspoons salt

3 tablespoons olive oil

2½ cups flour

1 cup cornmeal

Heat olive oil in large sauté pan. Add onion and garlic and cook 5 to 7 minutes over medium-high heat until onions begin to caramelize. Add 1 teaspoon vinegar, salt, pepper, and paprika. Meanwhile, place ½ teaspoon balsamic vinegar with sugar over tomatoes in large bowl and allow to marinate until time to bake.

In large bowl combine yeast with water and sugar. Stir well to combine. Set aside until foamy, about 5 minutes. Add salt, olive oil, and half of flour and mix well to thoroughly combine. Add 1 cup cornmeal and all remaining flour except ½ cup, and mix well with hands, working to incorporate flour little by little. The dough should be slightly sticky to the touch. Transfer dough to lightly floured work surface and knead for 5 to 7 minutes, adding additional flour as necessary to form smooth and elastic dough that is not too sticky. Transfer dough to lightly oiled 2 or 3 quart bowl and turn to coat with oil. Cover with damp towel and let rise in warm place until doubled in size, usually 1½ hours.

Divide dough into 2 portions and form into balls. Place on lightly oiled baking sheet and cover with damp towel. Let rest for 15 minutes, then transfer to lightly floured surface, shape as desired, and roll out to ⅛ inch thick. Transfer dough to pan of your choice (preferably a pizza stone) and prebake at 500 degrees for 5 to 8 minutes. On prebaked crust arrange tomatoes in circle, starting at outer edge and ending in center. Top with onions then cheese and herbs. Drizzle with olive oil and sprinkle dash of kosher salt and pepper on top. Bake until crispy and golden brown at 500 degrees, usually 7 to 12 minutes.

Dixie Line Olive Bread

Other than fresh french bread, this recipe relies on items you can stock in your pantry. (And in a pinch you can always use frozen bread from your freezer.) I like to use Boscoli Olive Salad from a company in Kenner, Louisiana. Of course, you can use other brands. I just can't vouch for them!

1 loaf french bread

Olive oil

1 (8 ounce) package chive and onion cream cheese (plain works, too)

Boscoli Olive Salad

Split the french bread halves open, brush with olive oil, and bake at 375 degrees for 10 minutes. Spread with 1 tablespoon chive and onion cream cheese and top with 1 tablespoon olive salad. Return to oven for 5 minutes. Slice into ¼-inch slices and serve warm with cream cheese.

Aunt Karen's Everlasting Applesauce Breakfast Muffins

These muffins are compliments of my husband's sister, Karen. The batter is easy to whip up and superconvenient to keep in the fridge for breakfast. And, as Karen reminds me, homemade muffins make great gifts!

4 cups flour

2 cups sugar

3 teaspoons allspice

2 teaspoons baking soda

½ teaspoon salt

1 cup butter, softened

2 eggs

2 cups applesauce

1 cup nuts (optional)

Stir together dry ingredients. Add wet ingredients and mix well. Fold in nuts if desired. Bake at 400 degrees for 10 to 12 minutes. Batter can be stored up to six weeks in airtight container in fridge!

Holiday Hurt Yourself Bread

I realize my recipes often have somewhat interesting names, but I'm going to have to ask you to reserve judgment until you taste this. You'll understand. The "hurt yourself" part named itself. I added "holiday" to remind myself that it just wouldn't do to serve this bread too often!

½ cup mayonnaise

½ cup softened butter

2 cups grated mozzarella cheese

1 teaspoon crushed garlic

1 teaspoon onion powder

1 cup finely chopped black olives

1 loaf french bread

Combine mayonnaise with softened butter. Add grated mozzarella. Stir in crushed garlic, onion powder, and chopped black olives.

Spread mixture over open halves of french bread and bake at 350 degrees for 10 to 15 minutes until bubbly. Slice bread into bite-size serving pieces and go ahead and hurt yourself. Seriously. (You can go back to your diet tomorrow.)

Belle Tip:

I don't mean to open a can of worms between two notoriously opposed factions, and I don't want to choose sides, but mayonnaise is not Miracle Whip and vice versa. Use that dastardly Miracle Whip at your own peril.

Parmesan Bread Bites

I make a sweet variation of this recipe called Monkey Bread, but it's more of a dessert. These little bites are quite a tasty alternative to the usual corn bread or french bread you're accustomed to serving with supper.

3 tablespoons and 1 teaspoon butter

1 teaspoon dill seed

1 teaspoon poppy seed

¼ teaspoon celery seed

1 (10 count) can refrigerator biscuits

¼ cup grated parmesan cheese

Melt butter and stir in seasonings. Divide refrigerator biscuits into fourths. Put them in plastic bag with grated parmesan. Shake to coat. Add seasoned butter and shake some more until well coated. Dump biscuit pieces into standard round Bundt pan and sprinkle top with another teaspoon melted margarine. Bake at 400 degrees for 15 to 20 minutes.

Beat the Heat Bread

I started calling this Beat the Heat Bread one summer day several years ago when I left my man outside grilling our meat while I went inside to put together the rest of the meal. The fresh spinach and lemon juice may have had a bit of help from the air-conditioning, but together they sure brought my temperature down!

3 teaspoons chopped garlic

2 tablespoons chopped fresh parsley leaves

½ cup (1 stick) unsalted butter, softened at room temperature

2 tablespoons fresh lemon juice

½ teaspoon black pepper

1 large loaf french bread

Fresh spinach leaves

1½ cups grated mozzarella cheese

Stir garlic and parsley into butter. Season with lemon juice and black pepper.

Slice french bread lengthwise. Brush flavored butter on both sides and layer with fresh spinach leaves. Top with mozzarella. Put slices back together, wrap whole loaf in foil, and put it on grill for 15 minutes (or in oven at 350 degrees for 15 minutes).

Summer's Shrimp and Feta Cheese PoBoys

A PoBoy can be very loosely defined as a sandwich stuffed with meat and served on baguette-style french bread, but there are countless variations on this popular recipe. New Orleans claims to be the birthplace of the PoBoy, and naturally we think the Big Easy has an airtight case. Here's my scrumpdillyicious PoBoy with fresh shrimp, veggies, and cheese.

1 pound fresh shrimp

½ bag frozen diced onion, pepper, celery blend

2 tablespoons butter

1½ teaspoons Old Bay Seasoning

1 loaf french bread

1 head romaine or large-leaf lettuce

3 tablespoons parmesan cheese

2 to 3 tablespoons feta cheese crumbles

Wash and devein shrimp. Sauté frozen onion, celery, and peppers in butter in cast-iron skillet. If I don't have the frozen blend on hand, I dice fresh veggies, but I'm all about keeping it simple. When veggies are softened, add shrimp and seafood seasoning. Cook another 2 to 3 minutes until shrimp is plump and pink.

Once shrimp are ready, spoon them with veggies over open-faced loaf of french bread. Top with lettuce leaves and sprinkle with parmesan and feta crumbles. Slice into sandwiches and serve!

Simplest Cathead Biscuits Ever

One evening I posted a picture of my big, fluffy cathead biscuits on social media. Mama had taught me how to make scratch biscuits eons ago, and I was wondering if it was a dying art or if most of my readers knew how to make biscuits. Well, I was floored! Floored, I tell you. I don't know how it happened, but we have a serious lack of edumuhcation (ed-u-muh-ca-tion: southern slang for educating someone, often used in conjunction with "Bless your heart") in this country. I am now doing my best to correct it. There are two ways for you to get up to speed: through this print version or with my handy-dandy YouTube tutorial. Just type in my name with "Cathead Biscuits." You'll find me! Every biscuit maker worth her or his salt probably has a preferred technique. What follows is how Mama taught me to make biscuits.

2 cups self-rising flour

2 to 3 tablespoons butter-flavored Crisco

1 cup buttermilk

2 tablespoons butter

Preheat oven to 400 degrees. Sift flour into large mixing bowl. (With today's flours, you may choose to sift or not to sift, but sifting delivers fluffier biscuits. Amen.) Cut 2 to 3 tablespoons butter-flavored Crisco into flour with fork until coarse crumbs form. (*Cutting* means to use a pastry blender or fork to blend flour and shortening. It'll look like cornmeal.) Add buttermilk and stir until ball forms. Stop working dough immediately or your biscuits will be packy. (*Packy* is one of Mama's words. It means dense instead of light and flaky. Packy biscuits are a no-no.)

Melt butter in skillet while pinching out biscuits. Divide dough in half and then halve each section again. You should be able to pinch out and roll 2 biscuits per section of dough for a total of 8 biscuits.

Now, here's another one of Mama's tips: as you form biscuits into balls, place them in melted butter, then turn them over. This will coat both sides and make a fine crust. Once you have placed all biscuits in skillet, press them down so they touch each other and the sides of the skillet. Bake for 12 to 15 minutes or until tops are brown. Make sure you butter 'em while they're hot!

That's it folks. Try it! You'll get better with every batch.

Belle Tip:

You can roll out your biscuit dough and cut it with a tin if you'd like, but Mama and I are pinchers.

"The butter has done slipped off his biscuit."

⚬⚬⚬⚬⚬⚬⚬⚬⚬⚬⚬⚬⚬⚬⚬⚬⚬⚬⚬⚬⚬⚬⚬⚬⚬⚬⚬⚬⚬

What began with high heels, pouring rain, and wet pavement ended with a night in the ER, a morning in the orthopedic clinic, and a verdict—fractured right arm. Excellent. Within hours I was scheduled to be in West Virginia speaking at The Greenbrier, known the world over as America's Resort!

On one hand, my remaining hand, I didn't want to cancel on these sweet people at the last minute. However, I was quickly realizing that I couldn't travel alone, because heretofore in my life I had apparently not required enough of my left arm. It knows nothing. Nothing, I tell you. Who you gonna call? 911 BFF!

Sometime later, my BFF and I were sailing through the skies on the first leg of our trip, with me seated eight rows behind Rhonda because we didn't get our tickets at the same time. Did I mention I was in pain? Surely no one will blame me for needing a distraction. Okay, maybe Rhonda, but I'm getting ahead of myself.

Now, what you should know about Rhonda is that she loves to fly, but she hates security. I mean, seriously hates it. Dreads it. None of us understand it, but Rhonda sweats like a terrorist when she goes through security. I was still thinking about Rhonda's neurotic aversion to security and how she was probably all settled in now with a smile on her face when I caught the eyes of our jovial flight attendant. I had pegged the man as a practical joker from the moment we entered the plane. (We people recognize each other. It's like we give off special vibes—think dog whistles.) On a whim, I waved my potential partner down and shared the details of what I must say was a brilliantly inspired prank that was still developing in my head. I knew he was in when his eyes began to gleam.

Within moments, under the gleeful eyes of several rows of interested folks who had overheard our conversation because I was born without the ability to whisper, the attendant approached my unsuspecting friend at the front of the plane. After confirming that she was Mrs. Perry, Mrs. Rhonda Perry, he informed her the cockpit had received information about a security breach and her name was involved.

Rhonda's face registered total shock.

The attendant asked her if she flew often. At this point, my poor buddy had no idea what the correct answer was as she had just recently been to both the Philippines and to Ukraine on separate mission trips, but she finally managed a weak reply. "Not that much."

The attendant assured her that this was probably the cause of it all, and some silly flag had just popped up, but then in an apologetic tone, he informed her that security personnel would still be waiting for her at the gate in Atlanta, and she would be detained for questioning.

(Breathe, Rhonda.)

It was time for the big finish. As the attendant apologized to Rhonda one last time for the trouble, he added that at least he had the name of the person who'd be conducting the investigation. And that's when my brilliant accomplice reached into his pocket and handed Rhonda my business card!

Boo-ya!

Rhonda spent the rest of that flight turning around and glaring at me. I couldn't see anything but her eyes over the seat back, but I had no problem understanding her message: "Soon as I can, I'm going to take your arm off and whup you with it."

What with security as it is in our world today, it's still hard for me to believe the attendant participated in my joke. But one of the funniest things about it all was that he and the pilot actually did wait for us on the tarmac that day, to present Rhonda with a little plastic pair of wings like those they give out to crying kids. Yep! BFF earned her wings! That should count for something—right?

I knew payback would be brutal, and it was. Rhonda has since repaid me for that prank in a dozen ways, all of them evil, and I'm sure Jesus is not proud of her. But that's another story. . . .

Berry Breakfast Bread

This bread is over-the-top good if you can score fresh dewberries from a ditch bank on the back forty, but it's also mighty delicious with fresh blueberries or blackberries from the store. Just don't start with frozen berries. They won't deliver the same results.

4 cups flour

2 cups sugar

2 teaspoons baking powder

1 teaspoon baking soda

1 teaspoon salt

4 eggs, lightly beaten

2 cups sour cream

1 cup vegetable oil

1 teaspoon vanilla

3 cups fresh dewberries (blueberries or blackberries)

Combine dry ingredients in small bowl. Set aside. Crack eggs into medium bowl and beat lightly. Stir in sour cream, vegetable oil, and vanilla. Add dry ingredients and stir. Fold in fresh berries. Pour batter into 9x13 casserole dish sprayed with cooking spray and bake at 400 degrees for 20 minutes.

I like to cut this breakfast bread into generous squares. (For the record, I've noticed that *generous* can be up for interpretation. I'm always trying to watch our serving sizes, but when I tell Phil he just needs a little something sweet to cleanse his palate, he says his palate must be larger than mine 'cause it takes more to cleanse it!)

Belle Tip:

When baking, combine dry ingredients and wet ingredients separately unless otherwise directed.

All sorrows are less with bread.

Miguel de Cervantes Saavedra

As you may have guessed, being on the road a lot gives me ample opportunities to stack up stories. But as much as I love the harvest of stories I get from road trips, it's the people I meet behind the stories that stay with me. Over time, and repeat visits, many of these folks begin to feel like family. I well remember my first visit to Bainbridge, Georgia, and the neighboring community of Climax. After speaking at a ladies retreat for Calvary Baptist Church, it was my great pleasure to accept an invitation from the girl who organized the event to join her large extended family for a Saturday evening fish fry.

The food and fellowship were flowing in excess, just like I like it, and I got to meet a fine old storyteller named Uncle Ed. Word has it that Uncle Ed was really just getting started that night, that he has a ton of stories where this one came from, and I believe it! Here's one of the beauties he shared with me:

Many years ago now, there was a man in their hometown named Bubba Newsome, whose habit it was to tell folks that he would "send up a few words for 'em," meaning that he would take their prayer requests to the throne. Now, there was another fellow in town by the name of Red Allen who, by all accounts, did less praying and more drinking. Every so often Red would fall completely off the wagon, disappearing for days at a time, down and out, and under the influence.

One day, Bubba and Red met up at the grocery store. After exchanging pleasantries, Bubba told Red that he'd send up a few words for him, to which Red lowered his voice and confided that he had just sobered up from a two-week drunk and he sure would appreciate the prayer.

At that news, Bubba stopped in his tracks and began his petition on the spot. "Lord," he began, "I'd like to have a few words with You about my friend, Red. He's gone and fallen off the wagon again. The poor boy just came off a two-week drunk—"

The good folks in Georgia are still laughing about what happened next. Red's head jerked up in horror. "For heaven's sakes!" he said to Bubba. "Don't tell *Him* that!"

No doubt Red was thinking he could get in enough trouble without any help from his friends. I get that. I've lived that.

The following account transpired during a trip to the beautiful historic city of

Charleston, South Carolina, to present at the Southern Independent Booksellers Alliance, also known as SIBA. Although the stay was far too brief, my family remains grateful that I wasn't detained for questioning, as there was that one time when I thought I might need an alibi.

That particular day I was heading to an author panel I was to moderate when I realized I'd left my notes in the hotel room. I suwannee! There was just enough time to run back up and retrieve them. I was in hasty transit when an author friend of mine by the name of River Jordan (I did not make that name up), texted me asking to borrow my big daddy hair dryer.

River had told me earlier—and this is the part I'll be using for an excuse—that our rooms were adjoining. I'm just saying, I distinctly recall her telling me that we should open the connecting doors between our rooms and have one big suite. Let the story continue.

I ran into my room, grabbed the necessary items, and opened the door that separated my room from the adjoining room. (In my haste, it may have hit the wall with a bang.)

Knock! Knock! Knock! I rapped loudly on the remaining door between the two rooms and used my and River's nicknames for each other to call out, "Cat! Open up! It's me, Dog!"

There was an immediate reaction from the other side. I heard feet running and the sound of a bolt lock. I waited impatiently. When the door didn't swing open, I knocked harder. "Open up, Cat! It's me, Dog!" And then I waited some more. And some more.

And that's when it hit me. River was wrong about our rooms connecting. The noise I heard wasn't my buddy trying to let me in. It was some other poor soul trying to keep me out.

I left as quickly and quietly as possible, praying I wouldn't meet security en route. It's not like I try to start trouble, y'all. It actually happens with very little effort at all.

"Besides, I meant well." Mama has said that for about as long as any of us can remember. When my sisters and I were teenagers, Mama was always using it to cover for people we were upset with if she felt we girls weren't being fair in our assessment of a situation. She drove us crazy saying, "She means well." Granted, we gave Mama ample opportunities to use her favorite platitude. One of us was always in a teenage tizzy about something someone did that we thought was rude, crude, and socially unattractive. We seldom thought they meant well, regardless of what Mama said.

I mention this in light of a couple of tiny social missteps of mine. Recently

I was on my way to participate in a book festival when I got a private message from a lady asking what time I'd be speaking. I didn't recognize her name, I didn't know how far she had to drive, and I didn't want her to be misled, so I replied that I spoke at four o'clock but she should know that I'd be sharing a panel with four other authors.

I didn't check my message before I sent it. I realized later that the autocorrect function on my phone had played a dirty trick on me. The message I had actually sent said I'd be "euthanizing" four other authors. While we authors do find ourselves trying to split the same pie of readers, I want everyone to know that I haven't resorted to offing the competition.

And in related news, around that same time, I sent my mother and my older sister a private message. In it I included a link to a certain medicinal cream another author had passed on to me that was supposed to help with all sorts of skin conditions—even the dreaded shingles. I haven't had shingles, but they have, so I sent them the link to the goods.

Sister Cyndie hit REPLY and wanted to know if I was serious or joking around again. That's the first time I realized the lotion was named Two Old Goats Cream. Tomboy honor.

Mama hasn't responded yet, but you do know what I'm going to tell her, don't you?

I meant well.

Southerners think words are like people. Peculiar people. Mix a bunch of them together and you can't tell what might happen.

ROY BLOUNT JR.

CHILI CHEESE CORN MUFFINS

My Chili Cheese Corn Muffins are a yummy way to serve corn bread, and they're super quick to stir up and slide in the oven. The jalapeños can be optional for your family, but they're expected and mandatory in mine!

1¾ cups self-rising cornmeal

1 cup flour

¼ cup sugar

¼ cup seeded and chopped jalapeño peppers

1½ cups whole milk

1 cup butter, melted

2 large eggs

1 cup grated sharp cheddar cheese

Preheat oven to 400 degrees and prepare muffin tin with nonstick cooking spray. Combine cornmeal, flour, sugar, and chopped jalapeño peppers in large bowl.

In separate bowl, stir together milk, melted butter, and eggs. Make small well in center of dry mixture and pour in milk mixture. Stir just until moistened and spoon into muffin tins.

Bake 20 minutes or until golden brown and serve 'em with supper—if you can wait that long.

Yields 12 muffins.

Pumpkin Bread from Kitchen Belleicious

Every fall I like to kick things off with delicious pumpkin bread topped with none other than our good friend cream cheese. The cream cheese topping is blended with a touch of browned butter and almond extract, making it irresistible and nutty, and the pumpkin bread is loaded down with classic fall spices of cinnamon, nutmeg, and cloves.

CREAM CHEESE TOPPING:

4 tablespoons unsalted butter

8 ounces cream cheese at room temperature

1 large egg at room temperature, lightly beaten

⅓ cup plus 4 tablespoons powdered sugar

1 teaspoon almond extract

PUMPKIN SPICE BATTER:

¾ cup brown sugar, lightly packed

2 large eggs

¾ cup pumpkin puree

2 tablespoons canola oil

1 teaspoon vanilla

1¼ cups flour

1½ teaspoons baking powder

¼ teaspoon baking soda

¼ teaspoon salt

¾ teaspoon cinnamon

½ teaspoon nutmeg

¼ teaspoon ginger

¼ teaspoon cloves

For topping, place butter in small saucepan over medium heat. Stir continuously for 5 to 7 minutes, until crackling and foaming have subsided and butter has browned and has nutty aroma. Transfer to large mixing bowl and allow to cool for 10 minutes. Add remaining topping ingredients to bowl and beat until smooth using stand or handheld mixer. Set aside.

For Pumpkin Spice Batter, preheat oven to 350 degrees and lightly grease 3 mini loaf pans with butter. In medium bowl, whisk together brown sugar and eggs until light and fluffy, then stir in pumpkin, canola oil, and vanilla. In separate bowl, whisk or sift together dry ingredients. Gradually stir dry ingredients into wet, being careful not to overmix. Divide pumpkin batter between 3 loaf pans, then pour cheese batter on top.

Bake until golden around edges, about 35 to 40 minutes, or until toothpick inserted comes out dry. Cool 10 minutes in pans, then remove from pans and transfer to wire rack to finish cooling.

Amen, Brother Ben, back your ears and dive in.

$\mathcal{H}$ere's another great travel story I nabbed from one of my author buddies. (Thanks, Lisa Wingate!)

Aunt Jerri and Uncle PJ are officially retired. They enjoy traveling and squabbling, and they have stories stacked up from both, like the time Aunt Jerri lost her wedding rings. The couple backtracked for miles and searched their vehicle high and low. Nothing. Aunt Jerri just knew those rings were history—until that last pit stop. She had barely gotten seated on the throne when she heard an unmistakable *plink, plink*. Her rings!

Aunt Jerri's momentary delight was interrupted by a horrific thought. What if this was one of those automatic toilets that flush as soon as you stand up? Being a woman of ample girth, Aunt Jerri found it difficult to turn and check without accidentally sending her rings to China. Sitting very still, she considered the situation from every angle. Clearly, there was nothing to do but go fishing on the spot. This, in turn, led to a lengthy wash job. By the time Aunt Jerri returned to the car, her man was fit to be tied, and the squabbling resumed.

Curiously, around that same time, Uncle PJ managed to misplace his sweetie in the middle of nowhere. As the story was told to me, it was nighttime and Aunt Jerri had been napping in the backseat while her man drove. She awoke to find they were parked at a convenience store. Aunt Jerri crawled out to tend to business without her purse or cell phone this time, expecting to find her man inside. It could've happened, but alas, the two of 'em passed like proverbial ships in the night.

Uncle PJ was miles down the road when his phone rang. Someone on the other end said he was calling on behalf of Uncle PJ's wife. "Who is this?" Uncle PJ demanded, suspiciously. "My wife's asleep in the backseat!" Then again, that person yelling in the background sounded mighty familiar. Uncle PJ reached behind him and checked the blanket. *Ruh-roh!*

The important thing here is that Uncle PJ did choose to turn around and face the music. No one ever said he got in a hurry about it.

Corn Bread Croutons

Some people might wonder why on earth a person would want to take perfectly good corn bread and make croutons out of it. I get that. The answer is, because they're delicious! But more importantly, because you make them with leftover corn bread. Once you've enjoyed a skillet of hot homemade corn bread straight from the oven, try repurposing that corn bread the next day into my tasty Corn Bread Croutons! You can use a corn bread mix, but I'm going to show you how to make scratch corn bread because it's so easy.

Butter for greasing skillet

1 cup cornmeal

1 cup flour

1 to 2 tablespoons sugar

1½ teaspoons baking powder

½ teaspoon baking soda

¼ teaspoon salt

6 tablespoons butter, melted

2 large eggs, lightly beaten

1½ cups buttermilk

Greek seasonings

Preheat oven to 425 degrees and lightly grease cast-iron skillet with butter. Place skillet in warming oven.

In large mixing bowl, mix dry ingredients. Cut in 6 tablespoons butter with fork. (This fork trick can be seen on YouTube. Just type in my name with "Cathead Biscuits." In lieu of the old-fashioned fork action, you can also use a pastry cutter.)

In separate bowl, mix lightly beaten eggs and buttermilk. Fold wet ingredients into dry ingredients, mix well, and pour batter into hot, buttered skillet. Bake until top is golden brown, 20 to 25 minutes. Inserted toothpick should come out clean.

The following day, cut day-old corn bread into ¾- to 1-inch squares. Sprinkle heavily with Greek seasoning (experiment with different seasonings) and toss bread with 3 to 4 tablespoons olive oil. Add salt and pepper to taste. Bake at 400 degrees for 15 minutes or until croutons begin to darken. The longer they sit, the crunchier they become!

Broccoli and Cheese Corn Bread

*I had the hardest time trying to decide if I should share my
Broccoli and Cheese Corn Bread with y'all (it's my favorite) or my
Okra and Tomato Corn Bread (my man's preference). In the
end I decided to share both and let y'all break the tie.*

1 (10 ounce) package frozen chopped broccoli

2 (8.5 ounce) boxes Jiffy corn bread mix

8 ounces sour cream

4 eggs

1 cup grated cheddar cheese

¼ cup (½ stick) margarine

Preheat oven to 375 degrees. Cook frozen broccoli in microwave with 2 tablespoons water. In large mixing bowl, combine broccoli with two boxes corn bread mix, sour cream, eggs, and cheddar. Melt a half stick of margarine in cast-iron skillet and let it get good and hot (this will put a nice crust on your corn bread). Pour corn bread mixture into hot skillet and bake for 30 to 40 minutes.

Okra and Tomato Corn Bread

*My man says this is southern cooking at its best, especially when
you use local veggies at the peak of their flavor. If you can't get fresh
veggies, use canned and drained vegetables. The water in frozen
veggies will alter the consistency of your corn bread.*

1 cup okra, chopped

1 cup tomatoes, chopped

1 cup chopped onion

1 (8.5 ounce) package corn bread mix

2 eggs

⅓ cup milk

Salt and pepper to taste

2 tablespoons butter

Stir okra, tomatoes, and onion into corn bread mix. Whisk in eggs and milk. Season with salt and pepper.

Pour into heated cast-iron skillet. Dot top with a few pats of butter and bake at 375 degrees for 30 minutes or until browned.

Cheesy Shrimp Spoon Bread

It may be called bread, but spoon bread doesn't have bread's texture. It's more like a pudding, hence its name! This one has cheese, peppers, and shrimp. Add your favorite salad, and you have a complete meal. What's not to love?

1 pound medium raw shrimp

1 small Vidalia onion, chopped

½ cup (1 stick) butter

16 ounces sour cream

3 medium eggs

1 (4.5 ounce) can chopped green chilies

1 (8.5 ounce) package buttermilk corn bread mix

1 teaspoon Cajun seasoning

Salt and pepper to taste

Dash My All Things Southern Comeback Sauce (see p. 145)

2 cups shredded Monterey Jack cheese with jalapeño peppers

Preheat oven to 375 degrees. Wash, peel, and devein shrimp. Chop into bite-size pieces and set aside. Sauté onion in butter until softened. Combine sour cream with eggs and green chilies in large mixing bowl. Stir in corn bread mix and season with Cajun seasoning, salt and pepper, and My All Things Southern Comeback Sauce.

Fold in shrimp and onion with all but ½ cup of cheese. Pour into casserole dish sprayed with cooking spray and top with remaining cheese. Bake 45 minutes. Let spoon bread rest before serving.

Belle Tip:

To devein shrimp, hold shrimp in one hand and use a sharp knife to make a shallow slit down the length of the back. Then remove the dark brown "vein" using the knife's tip.

CRAWFISH CORN BREAD

Put a pot of peas on the stove, throw a salad together, and stir up my Crawfish Corn Bread. Just like that, you've got yourself a mighty fine meal.

1 bell pepper, chopped

1 onion, chopped

2 stalks celery, chopped

2 tablespoons butter

Salt and pepper to taste

1 clove garlic, crushed

¼ teaspoon cayenne pepper

Cajun seasoning

Dash hot sauce

1 pound crawfish tails, peeled

1 (12 ounce) package corn bread mix

1 bunch green onions, chopped

1 (10 ounce) can Ro-Tel original diced tomatoes and green chilies

1 can cream corn

1 egg, beaten

Dash Worcestershire sauce

3 tablespoons butter

½ cup grated cheddar cheese

Sauté pepper, onion, and celery in butter in cast-iron skillet. While veggies are softening, season with salt, pepper, garlic, cayenne pepper, Cajun seasoning, and hot sauce. Add washed and drained crawfish tails, and cook 3 to 4 minutes.

Meanwhile, prepare corn bread mix according to package instructions and stir in Ro-Tel tomatoes, corn, and egg. Combine with veggies and crawfish and pour into casserole dish sprayed with cooking spray. Stir in Worcestershire sauce and bake at 400 degrees for 20 to 25 minutes. Top with melted butter and grated cheddar. Return to oven and broil until cheese is melted. Watch it carefully so it doesn't burn.

There's this thing I do that some people find odd. To be clear, I do a number of things that fall into that category, but for today's discussion, we'll stick with the one that concerns my trusty GPS, Mary Elizabeth III.

I've told my readers many stories in the past about my rocky relationship with Mary Elizabeth's predecessors. Not much has changed. Mary Elizabeth III and I have our ups and downs, too, mostly because Mary Elizabeth gets really snippy if I fail to take her every suggestion. She can also be, and I mean this in the nicest way, a tad vengeful.

Case in point: I was in a construction zone in downtown Dallas awhile back, and I literally thought the girl would implode under the pressure of trying to find our exit in the middle of all the demolition and detours. And yes, I may have laughed at her in the middle of her technological meltdown, but it was all in fun. I still say she was wrong for leading me to the wrong address in Waxahachie, Texas, the following evening, seeing as how I was almost late for my speaking engagement.

However, I chose to let bygones be bygones on our return trip because that's how Mama raised me and because I wanted to do that odd little thing I was telling y'all about before I digressed. I told Mary Elizabeth to take me home, and I left her little snippy voice on for the duration. I've had friends ride with me before, and they laugh when I let Mary Elizabeth continue to bark orders even after we're in familiar territory. I understand why they would think that. I suppose it is strange, but the thing is that I simply love that moment at the end of a road trip when I reach my long driveway leading to home sweet home on the banks of Lake Providence and hear Mary Elizabeth say, "You have arrived at your destination."

Those are sweet words indeed, but can I tell you that I'm anticipating a day when I will hear similar words heralding an immeasurably greater glory? It's gloriously true, for I live with the peace of knowing that heaven is my final destination, and one day I'll be welcomed there, not because of anything I have done, but because I have put my faith in Jesus, God's only begotten Son. This type of blessed assurance can be yours, too. There are plenty of people, yours truly included, who would be happy to show you the way.

For now we see only a reflection as in a mirror; then we shall see face to face.

1 CORINTHIANS 13:12 NIV

Cake Mix Pecan Cinnamon Rolls from Kitchen Belleicious

I can remember waking up to the smell of cinnamon rolls on Sunday morning before church and thinking, Oh, glorious day! I would literally jump out of bed so I could be the first one to the table! Cinnamon rolls need no introduction. They are the ultimate sweet treat for breakfast or dessert, drizzled with sweet cream and loaded with cinnamon and brown sugar. The irresistible aroma of the rolls can turn any day into pure bliss.

2 cups plus 2 tablespoons warm water

2 packages dry quick-rise yeast

4½ cups flour

1 box butter pecan cake mix

½ cup (1 stick) unsalted butter at room temperature, plus more for brushing

1 cup brown sugar

2 teaspoons sugar

4 tablespoons cinnamon

MAPLE VANILLA
CREAM GLAZE:

½ cup unsalted butter, melted

2 cups powdered sugar

2½ teaspoons vanilla

Pinch salt

¼ cup maple syrup

½ cup heavy cream

Combine warm water and yeast in large measuring cup. Allow yeast to dissolve, approximately 5 to 6 minutes. Mix flour and cake mix with hook attachment on stand mixer. Slowly pour in yeast mixture and stir and knead until dough is smooth, just slightly sticky. Place dough into lightly buttered bowl and cover with plastic wrap. Allow to rise and double in size. Divide dough in half and roll out each half into ½-inch thick rectangle. Spread entire surface of dough with softened butter using fingers or back of spoon.

Mix together brown sugar, sugar, and cinnamon. Spread over buttered dough. Repeat with remaining half of dough. Roll up tightly and cut into 1-inch slices. Place in buttered 9x13 baking dish and set aside to rise for another 15 to 20 minutes. It will make 12 to 15 rolls, depending on how you slice them. Brush a little melted butter over top of each roll and bake at 350 degrees for 20 minutes. Once rolls are slightly warm to the touch (not hot), generously drizzle with glaze and serve.

To make glaze, combine melted butter with powdered sugar in large bowl. Add vanilla, salt, and maple syrup. Slowly add heavy cream, whisking until smooth. As needed, add additional cream or powdered sugar to reach desired consistency. Glaze should coat back of spoon and still be easily pourable.

❧ 4 ❧

A Little Something Sweet

HOLIDAYS IN DIXIE

*I think as you grow older, your Christmas list gets smaller,
and what you really want for the holidays can't be bought.*
UNKNOWN

I realize Halloween kicks off the holiday season for most of the planet, but All Saints' Day (as it was historically known) doesn't move the needle for this belle. Sorry! Let the infamous heat and humidity of our Louisiana summers give the slightest hint of cooler fall temperatures, and my mind fast-forwards to harvest season on the farm and the soul-enriching act of giving thanks.

Most years, as I begin gearing up to lay down a holiday spread that would do my southern ancestors proud, my mind wanders to Thanksgivings past and hiding under my grandmother's dining room table with my sister Rhonda and our cousin Lisa. Our mission was to successfully emerge from beneath the draping white tablecloth to taste test the turkey without getting caught as our mamas trooped back and forth to the kitchen. I now realize we girls weren't nearly as sneaky as we liked to imagine. Those sweet women were

simply indulging our little-girl game in the gracious spirit of Thanksgiving.

Back then, loading up to go shopping after the family feast would've been unthinkable. These days it seems everybody and their mamas are headed to Wally World before the turkey gets cold. Here yet again, I find myself swimming against the tide. I've never been shopping on Black Friday for the same reason I don't pull my hair out at the roots. It sounds painful. But, if that's your thing, blessings on you, my Wally World Warriors. Be careful out there!

Those holiday celebrations at my grandparents' home are larger than life in my memories, as are my grandparents. I introduced my late Papaw Stone, a fun-loving Baptist preacher with a penchant for pranking, to my *All Things Southern* readers years ago, and I've since told a mess of stories on him to make my case. Papaw was not only my beloved grandfather and

96

the inspiration behind my own love of a good prank, he was also my hero in the faith.

Many years ago Papaw built an altar of twelve large stones in the woods behind his house, and the memory of that hallowed place is very special to me. So much so, that when I discovered just recently that his son, my uncle Rod, was not only in possession of those stones, but that he was willing to let me have one of them for my own prayer garden, I was like a gnat on caffeine. I couldn't focus on anything but getting to Rod's house to collect my stone. (Incidentally, Rod is my mother's younger brother, but he feels more like mine because he's only a couple of years older than me and he moved in with our family as a young man to farm with Papa. He is also Exhibit A for the old adage that an apple doesn't fall far from the tree.)

Rod called later that evening to remind me not to try and lift the heavy rock out of the car by myself. I promised him I was waiting on Phil to do that.

"Good," Rod said. "And, by the way, you do know the meaning behind Daddy's twelve stones, don't you?"

I told Rod I wasn't sure if they represented the twelve tribes of Israel or the twelve disciples.

"The twelve disciples," Uncle Rod replied. And then, because he is his daddy's son, he added, "I gave you Judas Iscariot."

Wonderful. I was hoping for Peter or John.

97

Homemade Caramel Corn

My Homemade Caramel Corn reminds me of the popcorn balls my Grandmother Rushing used to make, only we like this deliciousness served loose, like granola! It disappears as quickly as it comes out of the oven. In fact, we've taken to calling it Crack Corn around here. Yep, it's that addictive! See for yourself.

- 18 cups popped corn (3 bags microwave popcorn)
- 3 cups (16-ounce jar) dry roasted peanuts
- ⅔ cup butter
- ⅔ cup dark corn syrup
- 1¼ cups sugar
- 1½ teaspoons vanilla

Pop 3 bags of microwave popcorn. Pour into large roaster pan and toss with dry roasted peanuts. Set aside.

Meanwhile, prepare sugar mixture on stove by bringing butter, corn syrup, and sugar to boil. When candy thermometer reaches 260 degrees, stir in vanilla and pour over nuts and popcorn. Using two large serving forks and working quickly, stir sugar mixture and popcorn, trying to coat as much of the popcorn and nuts as you can. Cook in a 250-degree oven for 1 hour, stirring occasionally to continue distributing the sugar mixture. Let it cool, break it apart, and store in an airtight container!

Amazing Chocolate Caramel Cookies

This is as near to perfect as a cookie can get. It'll bake to a nice crunch around the edges while keeping a chewy center, thanks to the caramel pieces. Trust me. You'll make big points with these cookies!

1 cup (2 sticks) salted butter, softened

1 cup sugar

1 cup brown sugar

2 eggs

2 teaspoons vanilla

1 teaspoon baking soda

1½ teaspoons baking powder

¾ teaspoon coarse sea salt

2¾ cups flour

1½ cups semisweet chocolate chips

1½ cups caramel chips

Preheat oven to 350 degrees. Cream softened butter with sugars. Blend 2 minutes until batter is fluffy. Add eggs and vanilla. Continue blending 2 more minutes. Add baking soda, baking powder, and salt. Slowly add flour until incorporated into batter. Stir in chocolate chips and caramel chips. Drop batter by tablespoonfuls onto ungreased baking sheet. Bake 14 to 16 minutes. Cookies are ready when edges are golden brown. Allow cookies to cool for a few minutes on baking sheet—if you can.

All you need is love. But a little chocolate now and then doesn't hurt.

CHARLES M. SCHULZ

Brown Butter Maple Berry Skillet Cobbler from Kitchen Belleicious

Cobblers are one of our most popular southern desserts. Most people see a cobbler as a sweet, rich fruit filling topped with a crust, but I'm a bread-loving gal, so when I look at a cobbler, I see a delectable, sugary sweet, perfectly tender biscuit topping with a little bit of fruit underneath. Regardless of how you view it, this Brown Butter Maple Berry Skillet Cobbler is a keeper. The biscuit topping is taken to a new level with the brown butter, and the filling is rich in flavor thanks to basil, maple syrup, and nutmeg.

6 tablespoons unsalted butter

1½ pounds mixed berries, washed and well-drained

1 tablespoon cornstarch

1 tablespoon fresh basil leaves, roughly chopped

⅓ cup plus 1 tablespoon maple sugar, divided

1½ cups flour

2 teaspoons baking powder

½ teaspoon nutmeg

½ teaspoon sea salt

½ teaspoon fresh lemon zest

½ cup cold buttermilk

1 teaspoon vanilla

To make brown butter for baking, place butter in saucepan on medium-high heat to melt. Stir with wooden spoon as butter starts to foam then begins to bubble and turn brown. Scrape melted butter into small oblong pan or rectangular storage container and refrigerate for at least 4 hours or overnight. When the brown butter is solid again, slice into ½-inch cubes and set aside.

To make cobbler, preheat over to 400 degrees. Combine berries in large mixing bowl with cornstarch, chopped basil leaves, and 1 tablespoon maple sugar. Set aside.

In another mixing bowl, sift together flour, baking powder, nutmeg, salt, zest, and ⅓ cup maple sugar. Cut in cold brown butter (using fingers or pastry cutter) until mixture resembles coarse meal. Continue until some pieces resemble gravel. Blend together buttermilk and vanilla and add to flour mixture, stirring to make soft dough.

Lightly grease 4 miniature cast-iron skillets or one large cast iron pan or baking dish and fill with berry mixture. Drop biscuit mixture onto berries. Bake for 20 minutes or until fruit bubbles and crust is golden brown.

$\mathcal{N}$ow, I don't know how strong y'all are, willpower wise, but around here we can't eat Shellie's Cinnamon Apple Crisp without vanilla ice cream, which brings me to a certain public service announcement I've got on my mind:

Dear countrymen, lend me your ears. That No-Churn Ice Cream recipe all over the Internet is really good, slap-your-mama-if-you-dared good. And easy! One blender, three ingredients. Blend 2 cups whipped cream on high speed until it begins to get fluffy. Fold in 1 can sweetened condensed milk and a teaspoon of vanilla, and slide the whole thing in the freezer until it sets. It won't take long at all, a couple of hours tops, and you'll have some of the best homemade vanilla ice cream you've ever tasted. It's way better than dragging out the electric ice cream maker, rounding up the parts, and running to the store for rock salt because you never seem to have any on hand. And, it must be said: No-Churn Ice Cream slays the ice cream–making madness of my childhood.

It makes a belle feel old to realize that there are some among us today with zero memory of wrestling siblings and cousins for a turn at hand-cranking the ice cream, which the adults had somehow convinced us was fun. Score one for the big people, right? But thinking about the joys of No-Churn Ice Cream versus the old-fashioned hand-cranked delicacy led me to celebrate an entirely different type of sweet reward. Follow me here.

There have been far too many times in my faith journey when I've tried to hand-crank passion toward God into my distracted or distanced heart. I truly wanted to give God the type of worship He was worthy to receive, so when it wasn't there, I'd churn endlessly to try and make it happen. Not anymore.

Now when my heart is cold and I feel spiritually distant from God, I remind myself not to churn. Instead, I lean into Christ and gratefully acknowledge that He is ever with me, regardless of how I feel. I'm learning to keep my eyes off of me and my spiritual progress, or lack thereof, and keep them focused on Jesus. The results have been nothing less than life-transforming. No-churn praying is yielding the sweet relationship with Christ I once craved.

BELLE TIP:

For best results, chill your blender bowl in the freezer along with the paddle until it's supercold.

Okay, so I'm feeling compelled to tell y'all the whole truth about that Black Friday thing. It's not only that I'm allergic to shopping on Thanksgiving. I'm pretty much anti-shopping across the board.

To be clear, I enjoy browsing home accessories, and Lord knows I do love me a bookstore. My aversion is really more about clothes shopping than anything. During my growing-up years, Mama the Expert Shopper graciously brought clothes home for me to try on instead of dragging me around the mall. On that note, she spoiled me forever.

Bless her heart.

However, because God has a sense of humor, I gave birth to a female child who inherited Mama's shopping gene.

Bless my heart.

As a teenager, my daughter (recognized in these pages as Miss Kitchen Belleicious) developed the bizarre habit of designing a dress in her head for prom night and then trying to locate it in the stores. I kid you not. Her determination was legendary, and the resulting experiences can be credited with exacerbating what had been, until that time, my mild shopping aversion. The very memory is making me twitch, which I thought was an extreme reaction, too, until I learned of something called post-traumatic shopping syndrome. That's a condition whereby a person feels extreme agitation when shopping due to suppressed memories of earlier experiences.

My name is Shellie, and I have PTSS.

Though I'm now feeling quite vindicated, I refuse to allow my post-traumatic shopping syndrome from dampening my Christmas cheer. I mean, I honestly love decking the halls and buying toys for the grands. If the grown-ups get the short end of the stick, so be it, right? Shopping for mature people aggravates my symptoms.

Over the years, I've also learned to cope with my PTSS by eating chocolate throughout the shopping experience and indulging my love of people watching whenever I feel the stress building. Several years ago, I documented the following exchange in one of those big-box decorating stores between a couple who were clearly operating from different ends of the male-female logic spectrum. The shoppers in question were thirtysomethings, she stylishly underdressed in an "I just threw this on and I'm adorable" kind of way. Her man looked like he was set for a day of golfing with his buds. This may explain his impatience with how long it was taking his beloved to select a wicker basket.

"I don't want to be late," said Mr. Golfer.

"You have time," Cutie Patootie replied as she continued browsing.

Hopeful Golfer held up a basket. "How about this one?"

Cutie Patootie shook her head. "No," she said.

"It's got leather handles," her man announced. She shook her head again.

"You like leather," he insisted.

"I said no."

Desperate now, Hopeful Golfer resorted to reading the label. "But it's approved for residential use in California."

"Honey," Cutie Patootie said slowly, "we live in Texas."

You just can't argue with some people.

Should you decide that you, too, are suffering from post-traumatic shopping syndrome and thus choose to heed my stress-relieving tips, do be careful: people watching can backfire.

For illustration I give you the following exchange I once witnessed between two lovebirds who were struggling to stay in the holiday spirit without hurting each other. Man Person was so over the joy of shopping. He was ready to stick a fork in the day and call it done. Sweet Thang was determined to buy a gift for her mother. Man Person suggested perfume. Sweet Thang said they had bought her mother perfume last year and the year before that. "Perfect!" Man Person said. "It's a tradition now! Your mama loves tradition!"

Sweet Thang growled, oh yes she did. Tomboy honor. And then she said, "I don't care if we shut this place down. We're staying here until we find her a nice outfit."

I don't know what happened after that. I'm pretty sure I had a flashback to those shopping trips of yesteryear.

Let the record show that I agree with Man Person on more than one level. I like to say anything's a tradition if you do it twice. Here are some more of my family's favorite sweets. Try 'em! I'm willing to bet they'll find a permanent place on your go-to recipes list, too.

There is always, always something to be grateful for.

Unknown

Aunt Judy's Banana Nut Cake

Aunt Judy's Banana Nut Cake is super moist, and I may actually prefer it to banana nut bread because it's not as dense. But that's neither here nor there, right? You can't go wrong with either. Another thing I like about this recipe is that it's a dump and stir!

1 yellow cake mix

4 eggs

¾ cup oil

¼ cup milk

1 teaspoon vanilla

1 cup mashed bananas (about 2)

1 cup chopped pecans

Preheat oven to 325 degrees. Place all ingredients in large mixing bowl and stir well. Aunt Judy tells me her original recipe called for ½ cup of sugar, but one day Uncle Wayne surprised her by baking one while she was on her way home and he forgot the sugar. They discovered that it didn't hurt the flavor one bit, so I omitted it, too. Again, you make the call.

Pour batter into Bundt pan, spray with cooking spray, and bake for 55 minutes. Here's the most important step: plan to bake this cake when you can serve it warm out of the oven with piping hot coffee. And make sure you call me and Aunt Judy! Enjoy Aunt Judy's Banana Nut Cake, y'all. It's good eating, from our kitchens to yours!

Belle Tip:

When your bananas start to turn brown, resist the urge to toss them! This is when they make scrumptious desserts because the sugar has broken down! Just peel them and freeze that ripe fruit. It will be handy when you're in the mood for banana bread or Aunt Judy's Banana Nut Cake!

Scrumptious Skillet Cookie from Kitchen Belleicious

I was in Houston once, kissing on the baby beau czars, when my talented daughter whipped up a skillet cookie. I'd never had a skillet cookie at the time. Let's just say, I've been catching up ever since.

½ cup (1 stick) butter

½ cup brown sugar

½ cup sugar

1 egg

1 teaspoon vanilla

1½ cups flour

½ teaspoon baking soda

½ teaspoon kosher salt

½ cup dark chocolate chips

½ cup semisweet chocolate chips

Preheat oven to 350 degrees. Melt butter in cast-iron skillet. Add sugars and stir well. Remove from heat and let cool about 5 minutes before stirring in egg and vanilla.

Combine remaining dry ingredients and stir into sugar mixture. Fold in chocolate chips. Mixture will be thick, and it won't look like a cookie. Spread mixture with spatula as best you can in bottom of skillet. Bake for 15 to 20 minutes and try not to hurt yourself. It's not going to be easy; and of course, you know you'll need some vanilla ice cream, right?

12-Minute Microwave Pralines

The nutty goodness of pecans covered in crystallized sugar. Seriously? I'm in. Traditional pralines cooked on the stovetop can prove to be a tad tricky. Enter my microwave pralines. Even the novice cook can turn these out!

1 stick margarine

2 cups sugar

1 cup pecan halves

1 cup chopped pecans

1 teaspoon vanilla

1 (5 ounce) can evaporated milk

In microwave melt margarine in mixing bowl. Add remaining ingredients. Stir well. Microwave on high for 6 minutes. Stir, return to microwave, and cook on high 6 to 7 minutes more. Stir briskly until mixture begins to harden. Drop by tablespoons onto foil-lined baking sheet. Pralines will continue to harden.

MawMaw Lucy's Fudge Nut Muffins

When you need something warm and chocolaty, my late mother-in-law's Fudge Nut Muffins will definitely fit the bill! I make them in a regular muffin tin for family, but they also provide a pretty presentation in mini muffin tins for baby showers and other gatherings—and bonus, they'll go further!

1½ cups dark chocolate chips

1 cup (2 sticks) butter

¾ cup sugar

1 cup flour, unsifted

4 large eggs

1 teaspoon vanilla

3 cups chopped pecans

Preheat oven to 325 degrees. Melt dark chocolate chips with butter in double boiler over medium heat. Meanwhile, in large glass mixing bowl, combine sugar with flour. Stir in eggs and vanilla. Heads-up now, this is very important: don't use an electric mixer unless you want packed dry muffins! Stir until ingredients are mixed, do not over stir. Add melted chocolate and butter to glass bowl along with chopped pecans and, again, stir lightly.

Spoon into paper liners in muffin tin and bake for 30 to 35 minutes.

Pumpkin Spice Brownies

My Pumpkin Spice Brownies are taste tested and highly approved by my friends and family. The coffee extract is a surprise ingredient that adds the perfect bit of savory to all the sweet!

1¾ sticks butter, softened

2 cups (16 ounces) dark brown sugar

2 eggs

½ (15 ounce) can pumpkin pie filling

2 cups flour

2 teaspoons baking powder

1 cup chopped pecans

Dash salt

1 teaspoon vanilla

1 teaspoon coffee extract

Preheat oven to 350 degrees. Blend softened butter and brown sugar in food processor. Add eggs, pumpkin pie filling, flour, and baking powder. Mix well and stir in chopped pecans and salt. Stir in vanilla and—for a cool flavor—add coffee extract.

Pour into greased and floured 9x13 baking pan and bake for 35 to 40 minutes. You don't have to add icing, of course, but why not? I mean, *really*?

Here's a quick tip for those who choose it: Put 1 cup powdered sugar in small bowl and add 3 tablespoons milk and ½ teaspoon vanilla. You can add more milk or less, depending on how thick you like it. Let brownies cool, drizzle with icing, and serve.

Belle Tip:

And while I'm thinking about it, y'all, don't throw that extra pumpkin filling away. Put it in the fridge. You can add it to pancakes, chocolate chip cookies, soup, mashed potatoes, etc., etc., etc.

Most every southern family has at least one well-meaning aunt who spends the entire holiday hawking fruitcake with a line like this: "I've got a new fruitcake recipe for you. You'll love it. Scout's honor, it doesn't taste anything like fruitcake."

SHELLIE RUSHING TOMLINSON

Fruitcakes can be highly divisive. I'm sorry if that sounds harsh, but there's no sense beating around the bush. As it is, anti-fruitcake people are seriously underestimating the passion of the pro-fruitcake people. Case in point: in December 2014 someone paid $7,500 for an old piece of fruitcake from Prince William and Kate Middleton's April 2011 wedding. That's four, going on five, years, but who's counting? Fruitcake people are curiously proud of the dessert's shelf life.

I've had my own brushes with this seasonal hullabaloo. Several years ago, when Twitter was just a baby bird, I tweeted out what I intended to be an innocent holiday funny. I simply used my 140 characters to type, SOMEONE, SOMEWHERE IS DUSTING OFF A FRUITCAKE AND PREPARING TO SEND IT AROUND IN THE CHRISTMAS VERSION OF A CHAIN LETTER. JUST SAY NO. And, that's when the party started!

No sooner did I hit SEND than my social media circles began exploding with complaints from fruitcake lovers everywhere. The protest letters were easily divided into two camps. The milder respondents wanted me to know that I have obviously not eaten the right fruitcake. The more aggressive correspondents thought I should repent of my evil fruitcake hating ways or turn in my southern belle credentials. Wow. Tell me how you really feel.

For a while there it looked like I may need to go into hiding. I mean, did you know there is a Society for the Protection and Preservation of Fruitcake? Nor did I. Let's just say people are way more protective over their baked goods than I ever would've imagined. Honestly, I didn't know what to think about the heated reaction to my tweet, at least not at first. Then I began to notice how many of the fruitcake lovers were referencing their mothers' delicious fruitcakes. Suddenly it all made sense. By connecting the dots, I deduced that the pro-fruitcake people felt like I was disrespecting their mamas.

I, of course, would never do anything like that. And this is why, for the most part, I now try to avoid mentioning the controversial fruitcake. I do not want to fuel the great fruitcake divide. However, it is well known that I love a good story, and last Christmas season a fruitcake funny fell in my lap that I couldn't resist sharing, largely because it happened to one of the sweetest people on the planet. That would be my own beloved hubby.

Mr. Nice Guy and I were at my parents'. I was putting some soup on to simmer for their supper when I heard Papa offer Phil "some of the best fruitcake he'd ever put in his mouth—guaranteed!" Here's the thing, this man and I have been together for over three decades now. I know full well that he is not a fruitcake fan, so I couldn't help but grin when I heard Phil agree to try a slice, and I literally laughed out loud when Papa served Phil a generous slab of fruitcake and added, "Eat all that and I'll get you a bigger piece." Nice doesn't always pay.

Sometime later, Phil and I were driving home when I asked him if he'd like to order takeout for our own dinner and pick it up on our way through town.

"That's fine," Phil said, "but I'd rather go on home and get back out for it later—if it's okay with you."

I assured him I didn't mind waiting.

"Good," Phil said. "I'm not very hungry. I had to eat fruitcake."

And then, almost like an afterthought, Mr. Nice Guy added under his breath, "I don't like fruitcake."

That's my man, y'all, healing the Fruitcake Divide one slice at a time.

With Christmas comes our annual church program, directed by my BFF. Rhonda (also identified as Red in these pages) is an actress, playwright, set designer, and director extraordinaire. Over the years this one-woman drama company has written, directed, and starred in skits at our home church that have become the stuff of legends. Her offerings never fail to inspire and entertain, whether the actual productions or the rehearsals leading up to them. One such merry moment is sealed in the collective memory of all involved.

On a fine Sunday morning leading up to the annual production, my husband and I were helping the talented Miss Foster teach the three- to four-year-olds their own special routine. These littles were destined to be angels in the nativity scene. They wore long white gowns with beautiful feathered wings, and each of them held a battery-operated tapered candle in his or her wee hands. The candles were off during practice but the plan was for the lights to be lowered on the night of the big show so the wee ones and their candles could shine!

Miss Foster took her place in front of the cherubs so they could practice their routine by mimicking her motions. Cue the music. As Phil and I watched, Miss Foster made a large sweeping motion to the right. The angels followed suit, sort of. Then she made a grand sweeping motion to the left, and most of the angels mimicked her, except for Cullen the Angel Boy. That's when we first noticed the gleam in his eyes. Granted, Phil and I had no idea of the inspiration that had suddenly struck Cullen. We could never have imagined that little Cullen was now thinking to himself, *I know where I can put this candle.*

For there, directly in front of young Cullen, was the backside of Miss Foster, and it was all just too tempting. In the twinkle of an eye, Cullen the Angel Boy introduced Miss Foster to that candle, and we have video footage to prove it.

For some of us, Christmas 2014 will forever be remembered as the year Cullen the Angel Boy added his own verse to that sweet children's classic: *"This little light of mine. It's going where the sun don't shine."*

CynCyn's Buttermilk Pie

This pie comes compliments of my oldest sister, Cyndie. We call her CynCyn. It's a fitting contribution from her, too, seeing as how she lives on Buttermilk Road in northern Arkansas. (I can't make that up!) I told Cyndie she could call it her Crème Brûlée Hack because it tastes just like the fancy dessert—without all the fuss! CynCyn reminds us that this recipe needs to be cooked for one hour, no more, no less, to produce a pie that's semifirm but still moist. Oven temps vary, however. With mine, it takes about 45 minutes. Bottom line, just watch the pie those last few minutes to make sure it sets up without burning!

3 eggs, beaten

1½ cups sugar

3 tablespoons flour

Pinch salt

½ cup (1 stick) butter, melted

1 teaspoon vanilla

1 cup buttermilk

1 (9 inch) deep-dish pie shell

Beat eggs separately. Fold in dry ingredients. Stir in melted butter, vanilla, and buttermilk. Pour into pie shell. Bake at 350 degrees for 45 minutes to 1 hour.

Aunt Sandy's Red Cinnamon Candy

This recipe belongs to another of Phil's sisters. Aunt Sandy has been making her Red Cinnamon Candy for years. If you have trouble finding cinnamon oil in stores, buy it online. Using cinnamon extract will not deliver the same big flavor. If you're a cinnamon fan, this one's for you!

Powdered sugar
3¾ cups sugar
1½ cups light corn syrup
1 cup water
1½ teaspoons cinnamon oil
Red food coloring

Prepare baking sheet by sprinkling lightly with powdered sugar. Set aside. Mix sugar, corn syrup, and water in small saucepan. Heat on medium until candy thermometer reaches 300 degrees. Remove from heat and add cinnamon oil and enough red food coloring to turn syrup bright red. Pour immediately over powdered baking sheet and let harden. Crack into small, bite-size, irregular pieces.

Thanks, Aunt Sandy!

Belle Tip:

As an added bonus, the cinnamon oil will also clear up your sinuses if you inhale while you're adding it to the candy!

Carey's Old-Fashioned Caramel Cake

*This delightful cake comes compliments of my daughter-in-law, Carey!
Incidentally, Carey is the one who took all the pictures for this book.
Didn't she do a fabulous job? Carey makes this cake for all of our special
occasions, and we don't even have to beg. I mean, not a lot.*

1½ cups (3 sticks) butter

3 cups sugar

5 eggs

3½ cups flour

¼ teaspoon salt

½ teaspoon baking powder

1¼ cups buttermilk or whole milk

1 teaspoon almond extract

CARAMEL ICING:

1 cup (2 sticks) butter

2 cups (16 ounces) brown sugar

¼ teaspoon salt

⅔ cup evaporated milk

2 cups sifted powdered sugar

2 teaspoons vanilla

Preheat oven to 350 degrees. Cream butter and sugar. Add eggs one at a time and beat well after each addition. In separate bowl, combine dry ingredients. Add dry ingredients alternately with milk, then add almond extract. Beat until batter "ribbons." Pour batter into 3 greased and floured 9-inch round cake pans. Bake for 30 minutes and use toothpick to check for doneness. Cool layers on cake rack before icing. (I like to wrap them in plastic wrap and put them in the freezer for 45 minutes to make leveling the layers easier.) This cake can also be made in a 9x13 pan, which will need to bake for 45 minutes.

For icing, place butter, brown sugar, and salt in medium saucepan. Heat, stirring until brown sugar is well dissolved. Add evaporated milk and whisk until blended. Let bubble (at an easy boil) for approximately 4 minutes. Stir constantly to avoid sticking. Set hot mixture aside to cool for at least 20 minutes. Using mixer, beat in powdered sugar and vanilla. Mixture will turn lighter in color and caramelize. When desired consistency is reached, ice cake, including between layers. This cake is a bit of work, but boy is it worth it!

Shellie's Highly Favored Chocolate Lemon Bark Candy

I used to buy chocolate lemon bark candy in specialty stores every Christmas. Then, for some reason, it became hard to find, and there I was stuck with an addiction and no way to feed it. As they say, necessity is the mother of invention. There was nothing left to do but create my own recipe! I now share it with you along with an official proclamation. Yeah, I figure I should use this title of mine for good. Therefore, as the Belle of All Things Southern, I now proclaim that chocolate is the new tofu. You're welcome! And now, the recipe.

14 ounces old-fashioned lemon drops, crushed

1 pound white chocolate bark

4 teaspoons lemon extract

There are only three ingredients here, which means this recipe is supereasy, but I perfected the chocolate-to-lemon-extract ratio with trial and error. Take note: if you try to use anything less than 4 teaspoons of lemon extract, you're going to have white chocolate with lemon candy—not Chocolate Lemon Bark.

First, take a hammer to a bag filled with lemon drops and crush them into small pieces. (This is a good time to get out any buried aggression.) Set aside.

Melt white chocolate bark in double boiler and stir in lemon extract. Spread over waxed paper–lined baking sheet and sprinkle with crushed lemon candy. Refrigerate until set. Break candy up into bite-size pieces and enjoy.

We're all a little weird. And life is a little weird. And when we find someone whose weirdness is compatible with ours, we join up with them and fall into mutually satisfying weirdness—and call it love—true love.

ROBERT FULGHUM

And then there's Valentine's Day and all things love. Many, many years ago, when your humble hostess was a mere teenager, my friends and I sang along with the Everly Brothers as they crooned about the more painful aspects of human experience. Love hurts, love scars, love wounds and marks—you know, real happy-go-lucky type of lyrics. I no longer cotton to the mournful mood of those tunes, but they do remind me of a couple of good stories.

Like the old married couple who were still sparking well into their twilight years. Unfortunately, the husband began having some medical issues that led to his doctor laying down the law about intimate marital-type activities. Hearing that romance would now be life-threatening, the couple regretfully agreed to separate bedrooms. The husband would sleep upstairs; his sweetie would stay downstairs. This arrangement rocked along just fine, for at least a few weeks.

One long sleepless night the old man got up and headed down the stairs. To his surprise he found his wife headed in the opposite direction.

"Where are you going, old man?" she asked.

Her husband promptly replied, "I was headed downstairs to die. And where are you going?"

"I was headed upstairs to kill you."

I believe that's what they call counting the cost.

In other news of the heart, it hasn't been that long since I put my own beloved hubby's health at risk—completely unintentionally, of course!

It was harvest season, and my hardworking farmer had pulled something in his back that left him limping for days. Never fear, Shellie was here. For three straight mornings I sent him out the door with a good cup of coffee and two handy-dandy tablets of Aleve. Long about day three, Phil happened to mention that he'd been so sleepy the last few days that he could barely stay awake to drive the combine. You don't say? I slipped furtively to the medicine chest, hoping I hadn't done what I thought I'd done.

I did.

For three straight days, I'd given my hardworking farmer two Tylenol PMs in the a.m.—and sent him off to work with heavy equipment.

People like me, we mean well.

Where I'm From

I am from dark farming ground running alongside the Mississippi River, from Pixy Stix, Candy Straws, and freshly shelled peas.

I am from a matchbox house on a long dirt road soothed by an attic fan and noisy, rhythmic, surround-sound breeze.

I am from prized blue hydrangeas next to Grandma's front porch and scratchy green cotton stalks dripping with early morning dew and providing gracious canopy shades 'round my head while I hoed the weeds at their feet.

I am from Easter sunrise services, and that reminds me of a story—from Papaw Stone preaching Jesus to the faithful, from Mississippi's Charlotte Ann the Forestry Queen, and from Louisiana's James Ed, sired from tough-as-nails mountain people rooted deep in Kentucky.

I am from women toting a meat and three sides to white-unto-harvest fields where busy men nonetheless stopped work for midday feasts spread across tailgates, and from tuckered out children napping regularly in the footboards, vinyl seats, and warm back dashes of moving vehicles.

From "Straighten up and fly right" and drying it up so you wouldn't get something else to cry about.

I am from the second pew left-hand side, VBS, and "Deep and Wide."

I'm from the beauty of Natchez and moss-draped trees, from laughing, laboring common folk with nary an aristocrat to claim, from corn bread crumbled in cold milk and fried bologna cut as thick as your finger.

From the gritty grandmother birthing number ten once the nightgown of toddler number nine was secured 'neath the bed's heavy wood frame, his sticky, honey-coated baby fingers occupied with a feather. I'm from this anchored boy child who grew up and chose to be my dad after a blood parent opted for freedom over his young wife and stair-step girl children.

I am from black-and-white photos heaped in cardboard boxes, hymns sung around well-worn pianos, family stories told more times than a few, and long, tall shadows cast by each generation challenging the next to remember who we are and where we're from.

SHELLIE RUSHING TOMLINSON

We're all about Independence Day in this family. Consequently, our annual celebration is too big to be contained in one day. We prefer to take the entire first week of July to celebrate our country's birthday! There are no rules stating you have to get sunburned and eat your weight in barbecue, fried corn, and peach ice cream. It's just understood, or misunderstood. While you're making that call, I'll close out this chapter with a great small-town Fourth of July funny about Opal and Jessie, a couple whose names have been changed to protect the not-so-innocent.

Opal and Jessie are from a small town where Jessie serves as director of the Ambulance District. Occasionally, Opal and Jessie will grill out and invite whoever's on duty to drop in should they find a spare minute. This particular Fourth of July, Jessie was just pulling the barbecue off the grill when a call came in from the station. It was an emergency OB—someone was giving birth! Now, this would have demanded urgency under any conditions, but their small rural hospital doesn't deliver babies. With everyone aware that transporting the laboring mom to a nearby town only increased the odds that the wee one might decide to make a grand patriotic entrance en route, the crew rushed to the scene, trying not to think about barbecue.

Arriving at the emergency address with lights flashing and sirens wailing, they wasted no time backing the ambulance in, unloading the stretcher, and heading for the door, which is where they found an elderly lady with a very puzzled look on her face. She got even more confused when they inquired as to the condition and the whereabouts of the birthing mother.

"Fellows," she said. "It's just me here!"

Jessie's crew exchanged glances. "Ma'am," one of the guys said, "are you saying you didn't call 911 and tell 'em your water broke?"

The sweet old belle shook her head, "Oh, yeah, I called 911 because my pipes burst and flooded my house. But my water—fellows, my water done broke a long time ago."

I understand the crew did eat barbecue that day, eventually. And the dispatcher—I think he got some cold ribs and some good natured ribbing, too. I get that. What with the holiday and all, I think it was the all-American thing to do.

We on this continent should never forget that men first crossed the Atlantic not to find soil for their ploughs but to secure liberty for their souls.

ROBERT J. MCCRACKEN

Cathy Wedel's Layered Lemon Dessert

*I was at the right place at the right time to snag this seriously good recipe.
I had dropped in on Mama and Papa about the same time they got a
visit from neighbor and longtime friend Cathy Wedel, who came bearing
dessert! Cathy and her husband used to run the famous Old Dutch Bakery
here in my hometown. We, their loyal fans, still dream about them
opening up again. But, I digress. Cathy said I could share her
Layered Lemon Dessert with y'all, and time's a-wasting.*

CRUST:

½ cup (1 stick) butter

1 cup flour

FILLING:

1 (8 ounce) package cream
cheese

½ cup powdered sugar

1 (8 ounce) tub nondairy
whipped topping

TOPPING:

2 cups sugar

¼ teaspoon salt

⅓ cup cornstarch

2 cups water

3 eggs, beaten

¼ cup lemon juice

¼ cup vinegar

1 tablespoon butter

1 tablespoon lemon extract

Preheat oven to 350 degrees. For crust, add chilled butter to flour and blend in food processor until fine. Spread in bottom of 9x13 casserole dish, bake for 15 minutes, then set aside to cool.

For filling, mix cream cheese with powdered sugar before folding in nondairy whipped topping. Spoon over cooled crust. Chill.

Meanwhile, prepare lemon topping. Combine sugar, salt, and cornstarch in medium saucepan. In bowl combine water, eggs, lemon juice, and vinegar. Gradually add to dry ingredients in pan over medium heat until mixture begins to thicken. Add butter and lemon extract. When thick, cool at room temperature. Pour lemon topping over filling and chill.

Big C's Peanut Butter Pie

Big C would stand for Charlotte, my own dear mama. It's just another name the Queen of Us All goes by. So, here's the thing. I didn't even know I liked peanut butter pie until this past year when I found it in one of her old cookbooks! I don't remember her making it before, but she said she used to stir it up all the time. I'm now wondering what else she is holding out on!

8 ounces cream cheese

1 cup powdered sugar

½ cup peanut butter (I like chunky!)

½ cup milk

1 (8 ounce) tub nondairy whipped topping (I used sugar-free)

Graham cracker crust

Whip cream cheese in food processor with powdered sugar and peanut butter. Add milk and nondairy whipped topping. Once everything is well blended, spoon into graham cracker crust. If you can, leave it in the freezer overnight without anyone snitching a piece. I'll be honest—if they've had it before, that's going to be the hard part.

This is optional, but if you have a little chocolate to shave over the top, by all means do so. It only makes it better!

Save room for dessert.
SOUTHERNER SAYING

Aunt Marleta's No-Fail Christmas Fudge

Everyone loves fudge, but not all fudge recipes love us in return. Some of them will up and refuse to set despite a cook's best efforts. And that's why you need Aunt Marleta's No-Fail Christmas Fudge in your arsenal. It's a three-step version that has never let me down.

3 cups semisweet chocolate chips

1 can sweetened condensed milk

Scant teaspoon salt

1 teaspoon vanilla

1 cup chopped pecans

1. Stir chocolate chips, sweetened condensed milk, and salt in saucepan. Heat on stovetop over medium-low heat just until chips melt. Remove.

2. Stir in vanilla and pecans.

3. Pour into foil-lined square baking pan and refrigerate. Once fudge sets (about 1½ hours), turn foil over onto cutting board and slice into squares. Voilà! Share and share alike.

Shellie's Cinnamon Apple Crisp

Fall weather makes me think of piles of leaves, big orange pumpkins, and apples! Try my Cinnamon Apple Crisp when the weather starts cooling down in your neck of the woods.

8 cups apples, peeled and sliced (about 15 medium-size apples)

¾ cup sugar

1 cup flour, divided

3 teaspoons cinnamon, divided

½ cup water

1 cup quick oats

1 cup brown sugar

½ teaspoon baking soda

¼ teaspoon baking powder

½ cup (1 stick) butter, melted

½ teaspoon apple pie spice

Preheat oven to 350 degrees. Peel, core, and slice apples. Layer in bottom of casserole dish. I like to use a variety of apples, but this recipe works with whatever you have on hand. Combine white sugar, ½ cup flour, and 2 tablespoons cinnamon. Sprinkle over apple slices. Pour ½ cup water over this.

Combine oats with remainder of flour, brown sugar, and 1 teaspoon cinnamon, baking soda, and baking powder. (Can you tell I love cinnamon?) Stir in melted butter and crumble over apples. Sprinkle dish with apple pie spice for good measure. Bake for 45 minutes.

Old-Fashioned Oatmeal Pies from Kitchen Belleicious

Who didn't fall in love with the chewy, delicious Little Debbie Oatmeal Pies as a child? (Kitchen Belleicious confession: I used to hide these store-bought pies from my little brother because he could polish off a box in a heartbeat!) With creamy goodness in the center and the chewy yet firm oatmeal cookie on the outside, they are simply delicious. I am drooling just thinking about them. Now get in the kitchen and let this homemade version bring you back to your childhood.

COOKIES:

- 1½ cups plus 2 tablespoons whole-wheat flour
- 1 cup plus 2 tablespoons flour
- 1 teaspoon baking soda
- ½ teaspoon kosher salt
- ½ teaspoon cinnamon
- 3 cups old-fashioned cooking oats
- 2 sticks unsalted butter, room temperature
- 1 cup brown sugar
- ½ cup sugar
- 1 large egg
- 2 teaspoons vanilla

CREAM FILLING:

- 4 tablespoons unsalted butter, softened
- 2 cups powdered sugar
- 2 tablespoons heavy cream
- 1 teaspoon vanilla

Preheat oven to 375 degrees. Line baking sheets with parchment paper or silicone liners. Whisk together flours, baking soda, salt, and cinnamon. Stir in oats. Set aside.

Using electric mixer, beat butter and sugars until creamy. Add egg and vanilla. Mix well. Gradually add flour mixture, stirring until well blended. Drop dough by rounded tablespoonfuls, 2 inches apart, onto prepared baking sheets. Bake 8 to 10 minutes. Cool on pan 2 to 3 minutes, then remove to wire racks to cool completely.

Filling: Combine all ingredients in medium bowl. Using mixer on low speed, beat until combined. Increase mixer speed to high and beat until light and fluffy. Spread about 1 tablespoon filling over bottom side of half the cookies. Top with remaining cookies so that bottoms are facing filling. Yum!

Aunt Debbie's French Market Doughnuts

Aunt Debbie is my husband's middle sister. Her French Market Doughnuts will make you feel like you're in the Big Easy feasting at the famous Café du Monde. Debbie has this recipe down to a few simple steps that anyone can follow. Enjoy a taste of New Orleans without leaving your home sweet home.

½ cup shortening
½ cup sugar
1 teaspoon salt
1 cup boiling water
1 cup evaporated milk
1 package yeast
¼ cup warm water
2 eggs, beaten
7½ cups flour

Add shortening, sugar, and salt to mixing bowl. Cover with boiling water. Add evaporated milk. Stir. Dissolve yeast in ¼ cup lukewarm water and stir into mixture. Stir in beaten eggs and 4 cups flour. Beat well. Add remaining flour a cup at a time until soft dough forms. (You may have a little flour left over.) Dough is ready when it starts pulling away from bowl, but it will still be sticky. Place in greased bowl and grease top of dough with shortening. Cover with damp cloth and keep in refrigerator until ready for use.

To prepare doughnuts, roll dough to ¼ inch thick. Cut with knife into strips and fry in just enough oil to cover your doughnuts. Fry doughnuts about a minute on one side; flip and continue frying until slightly brown. Drain on paper towels and sprinkle with powdered sugar. Note: you don't have to let this dough rise before frying.

Belle Tip:
Never use hot water to dissolve yeast!

❧ 5 ❧

SOUPS, SAUCES, AND TOPPINGS

PUBLIC SERVICE ANNOUNCEMENTS FROM THE BELLE

Where facts are few, experts are many.
DONALD R. GANNON

Over the years here at *All Things Southern*, my body of work has expanded in ways I never could have imagined. For instance, I've become something of a behavioral expert. I use the term *expert* very loosely, but it's true nonetheless. I regularly research and document behavior that my colleagues in the field are either ignorant of or refuse to address. You can brush up on many of these findings in my humor books. Like male speaker syndrome (MSS), for example. This is a widespread condition that causes men to sweat when ordering from fast-food speakers.

Along with documenting some of these lesser-known syndromes, I also give regular public service announcements in an effort to keep my busy readers informed of current events that may otherwise slip by them. And on that note, ladies, belles, countrywomen, lend me your ears. We've got trouble.

A group of experts claims to have proof that we are our men's greatest health hazards. Not disease, not stress at work, not even accidents. It's you and me. We're nagging them to death.

My man and I were watching the news together when the story broke. Phil tried not to grin. He failed. However, he has since released his own statement that reads, "This study is bogus, and the men who conducted it should be ashamed of themselves." No, I did not have anything to do with that, and I don't know why you'd ask.

The news anchor team Phil and I were watching that morning was sharply divided—along gender lines. The female anchor was skeptical, but Mister Anchor doubled down. Not only did he give the report considerable airtime, but he kept insisting the whole thing was solid science. I wanted to tell him to move on in case his wife happened to be watching and he and science found themselves sleeping on the couch.

Let the record show I've tried to be objective about this report. I even called Papa for a quote. Papa said the study was nonsense, and he would elaborate but Mama needed him to take out the trash and he didn't want her to have to ask twice. Whatever, Papa.

I also brought it up at a church speaking engagement to document the audience's response. As of this writing, I can only conclude that whether or not the claim is valid, there are those from both sides buying into it.

Ironically, the men of the congregation had waited tables for us ladies that evening. Afterward they were gathered at the back of the room listening to my remarks when I brought up these purported correlations between nagging and premature death. One of the ladies twirled around and grinned at her husband. He returned her smile, but I was told that after she turned back around, the man met the eyes of his closest friends and solemnly opined, "Fellows, I'm living on borrowed time."

Bless his heart.

The fear of the LORD is the beginning of wisdom,
and the knowledge of the Holy One is understanding.
PROVERBS 9:10 NASB

They say there's a comedian in every crowd. If that's true, my family is way above average. I may be the most public storyteller of the bunch, but we have more than our share of comedians. One day my oldest sister, Cyndie, called and launched into a conversation with neither a how-are-you or a fare-thee-well.

"Shellie," she said, "do you remember that joke where Boudreaux asks Thibodaux if he had a million dollars, would he give him a hundred—and Thibodaux says sure he would?"

"Yes," I said. "Why?"

Cyndie rushed ahead, "So, Boudreaux asks Thibodaux if he had a thousand dollars would he give him ten?"

I knew the joke. I also knew Cyndie was bound and determined to tell it all.

"So," Cyndie said, "Thibodaux says yes, if he had a thousand dollars, he'd give Boudreaux ten. It goes on that way until Boudreaux finally asks Thibodaux if he had two dollars would he give him one of 'em?"

Cyndie and I finished the joke in unison, "And Thibodaux says, 'Dad-blast it, Boudreaux, you know I got two dollars.' "

After we laughed together, I asked Cyndie why we were telling Boudreaux jokes. Quick as lightning, my sister switched gears. She told me she was going in for some kidney tests. "I really think I'm okay," she said. "I've prayed about it and everything. But I was wondering, just to put my mind at ease, if you had two good kidneys, would you give me one?"

"You're serious," I said. "You're asking me for a kidney right here, like this?"

"You're my sister, aren't you?"

I told Cyndie I was pretty sure people didn't handle this kind of thing over the phone. "Why," I said, "it'd be like me telling this story on the radio or in one of my books right in front of God and everybody."

"Suit yourself," my sissy replied. "I don't care. Just tell me, if you had two kidneys, would you give me one?"

Dad-blame that girl. She knows I have two kidneys.

You-Won't-Miss-the-Meat Veggie Chili

*I saw you roll your eyes at that title. My man had the same reaction
until he tasted it! Mr. Where's the Beef? now loves this chili!
Try it, and I may make a believer out of you, too!*

1 bag frozen onion, pepper, celery blend

1 tablespoon olive oil

1½ tablespoons minced garlic

1 (15 ounce) can kidney beans, rinsed

1 (15 ounce) can black beans, rinsed

1 (16 ounce) can chickpeas, rinsed

1 (15 ounce) can tomato sauce

2 medium jalapeño peppers, finely chopped

1 cup frozen corn niblets

1 (16 ounce) jar salsa

3 cups water

⅓ cup chopped cilantro

2 to 3 tablespoons chili powder

2 teaspoons ground cumin

Salt and pepper

Suggested toppings: sour cream, grated cheese, and chopped green onions

Sauté onion, pepper, celery blend in olive oil. Add garlic after veggies begin to soften. (Adding the garlic earlier will produce a bitter flavor.) Combine beans, chickpeas, tomato sauce, jalapeño peppers and corn in large dutch oven. Add salsa and water. Heat to boiling. Stir in veggies when tender. Season with cilantro, chili powder, and cumin. Add salt and pepper to taste. Once chili begins to bubble, turn heat to low and cook 45 minutes to an hour. Flavors intensify the longer it simmers.

Serve warm topped with sour cream, grated cheese, and chopped green onions.

Mama's Simply Delicious Hamburger Soup

I've been eating Mama's Hamburger Soup all of my life. When I was a newlywed, it may have been one of the first recipes I called home about. Mama gave me the straightforward instructions, and it's been a go-to comfort food around this house ever since. This makes a big pot, but you'll be happy about that, too. It's just as good the second day.

1½ pounds ground beef

1 onion, chopped

4 to 5 medium potatoes, chopped

1 (1 pound) bag frozen soup veggies

2 cups beef stock

1 (28 ounce) can tomatoes

2 (15 ounce) cans tomato sauce

1 teaspoon minced garlic

1 bay leaf

1 teaspoon oregano

1 teaspoon cayenne pepper

Salt and pepper to taste

Brown meat with onions. If you have a lot of grease when the ground beef is browned, just lift some of it off with a spoon, but it's not necessary to drain the entire pot unless it's supergreasy. Add potatoes, remaining vegetables, beef stock, tomatoes, and tomato sauce. Season and cover. Simmer until all veggies are soft. Remove bay leaf and serve piping hot!

Belle Tip:
Try experimenting with new flavors of tomatoes and tomato sauces, like tomato sauce with basil, garlic, and oregano.

Mexican Tortilla Soup

I'm a big fan of the new Swanson flavored broths. This recipe came from a box of Mexican Tortilla Flavor Infused Broth—with a few of my little tweaks—and it hit the spot! Stir it up for your hungry bunch and serve with your favorite bread!

2 cups diced onion, pepper, celery blend, frozen or fresh

2 tablespoons butter

5 to 6 chicken breasts, roasted and deboned

Cajun seasoning

1 (32 ounce) carton Swanson Mexican Tortilla Flavor Infused Broth

2 cups frozen corn

1 teaspoon white vinegar

1 (6 ounce) can tomato paste

1 (15.5 ounce) jar salsa

1 (15 ounce) can black beans, washed and drained

2 tablespoons crushed jalapeños

2 teaspoons minced garlic

Suggested toppings: grated sharp cheddar, diced green onions, chopped cilantro, sour cream

Sauté onion, pepper, celery blend in butter. Rub chicken breasts with Cajun seasoning and roast in 350-degree oven for 45 minutes. Pull meat off bones and shred into bite-size pieces.

To get your soup on, scoop sautéed veggies into large soup pot and add broth, corn, vinegar, tomato paste, salsa, and black beans. Stir well and add pulled chicken. Season with diced jalapeños and minced garlic. Heat to boiling, reduce heat, and simmer 30 minutes to an hour for flavors to mingle. That's it! Serve over a bed of chips with your favorite toppings. I use grated sharp cheddar, diced green onions, chopped cilantro, and sour cream!

I don't know what it is about food your mother makes for you, especially when it's something that anyone can make—pancakes, meat loaf, tuna salad— but it carries a certain taste of memory.

Mitch Albom

In my unexpected role of behavioral analyst, I'm often called upon to be the voice of reason for the *All Things Southern* community. (This is frightening on a number of levels, but I'm resisting the urge to digress.) For instance, not long ago some concern was voiced among my girlfriends as to whether or not our generation was in danger of losing a long-held and iconic trait of the Southern Mamahood!

The sober suggestion had been made that we belles are growing increasingly incapable of properly portraying the long-suffering southern mama, defined by yours truly as "one who is so saintly as to suffer on behalf of her offspring without bothering them with her pain—at least not in an overtly obvious way." The long-suffering southern mama is much too subtle for that.

I spent some time studying this special skill set, and I'm happy to share my conclusion with y'all, but first, let's look at a defining illustration involving one of the experts to make sure we're all on the same page.

One of my girlfriends, who asked to remain anonymous in this chat, left the country for a brief mission trip. The trip meant she would be without cell phone service for almost a week. Her husband was concerned about not being able to stay in touch with her, as were her children, but none of them summed up the impact this trip might have on their lives quite as succinctly as her long-suffering southern mama.

"Now, don't you worry one bit about me while you're gone," her long-suffering southern mama said. This while my harried friend was making arrangements for her husband, kids, pets, and anybody else who might be affected by her absence as she simultaneously packed, got a half dozen immunizations, made her lists, and checked 'em twice.

"If I die while you're gone," her long-suffering southern mama continued, "I've given orders to everyone that I don't want anyone calling you and messing up your trip. There's no sense in you hurrying home for my funeral. I'll still be dead when you get back."

Be at peace, my fellow belles. You, too, can one day be a long-suffering southern mama, but that sort of skill level can't be rushed, not even with genes as strong as ours. It has to be developed over time.

I don't know what class is, but I can tell when one has it. You can tell it from a mile away.

BEAR BRYANT

***

Some of my PSAs are more critical than others. I'm as serious about this next one as Elvis was about his blue suede shoes. Brace yourselves, seasoned matriarchs and those in training. I have learned that there are people mailing out something called the noninvite along with their traditional wedding announcements. These noninvites read, "We're getting married. You're not invited."

I know you need time to let that sink in, y'all, but we'll need to act quickly to head this off. I'm told the noninvite is supposed to gently let people know whether or not they're invited (because apparently not getting an invitation isn't a big enough clue), but I think it sounds like the rudest nana-nana-boo-boo of all time. I know first graders with better manners.

I suspect the real motive is securing a wedding gift from more people, but I don't think the participating brides have thought this through, as I don't see it working out well. As my friend Paulette said, "Sending my family and friends a noninvite might buy you a prize, but it won't be anything listed on your registry." True.

The noninvite idea needs to be squashed before it gains a footing and seeps into the larger culture. Can you imagine living in a world where you could get a note that reads, "We're cooking barbecue, but you can't smell it."

Girls, we all realize that making out a guest list can drive a belle straight-running crazy. If you are genuinely concerned that you might offend someone, let me put your mind at rest. You will. Offend someone, that is.

Feel better?

Indeed, you'll inevitably overlook people who really do want to come to your wedding, and you'll invite others who'll wonder why on earth they're on your list. In the first scenario, just follow the time-honored tradition of our mothers, their mothers, and their mothers before them. Plead ignorance.

"Of course you were invited! You mean you didn't get your invitation?"

Unlike the noninvite, the ignorance plea is foolproof.

Heartiest Cheesy Broccoli Soup on the Planet

Here's the backstory on my Cheesy Broccoli Soup. I was keeping my grands one evening, and they love broccoli and cheese soup. My man does, too, but that particular evening he had his mouth set for a supper he could sink his teeth into. So I created the following meal that made everyone happy!

REGULAR SOUP:

½ onion, minced

4 tablespoons unsalted butter, softened

1 teaspoon minced garlic

4 tablespoons flour

2 cups half-and-half

1 to 1½ (32 ounce) cartons chicken broth

1 large carrot, peeled and chopped small

2 heads broccoli, cut into florets

2 cups mushrooms, washed and sliced

8 ounces grated sharp cheddar cheese

4 ounces Velveeta

¼ teaspoon nutmeg

2 bay leaves

BEEFED-UP OPTIONS:

4 to 5 medium potatoes, washed and cut into bite-size pieces

Bread bowls

Rotisserie chicken from grocery store

Sauté minced onion in melted butter. When onion is tender, add minced garlic and flour. Gradually stir in half-and-half and chicken broth. Adjust liquid to your preference.

Wash and peel carrot, prepare broccoli, and slice mushrooms. Stir veggies in with cheddar and Velveeta. Season with nutmeg and bay leaves. Simmer on low for 30 minutes or until you're ready to eat.

For a heartier version of this soup, add potatoes that have been washed, diced, and parboiled along with shredded rotisserie chicken from the big-box store. Season with salt and pepper and serve in bread bowls. I told y'all I pumped it up!

Belle Tip:

When making gravies and sauces, add your thickening agent to your liquid and not the other way around to avoid lumps!

THREE-BEAN SOUP

To be perfectly honest, the biggest difference between my three-bean soup, four-bean soup, and five-bean soup generally comes down to how many varieties of beans I have on hand. Keep your pantry stocked with cans of beans and broth, and keep a reserve of ground beef in your freezer, and you'll never be more than 30 minutes away from a tasty soup on a cold day!

2 pounds ground beef

1 onion, chopped

1 (15 ounce) can black beans

1 (15 ounce) can kidney beans

1 (15 ounce) can pinto beans

1 can chopped green chilies

1 (28 ounce) can stewed tomatoes

1 quart beef broth

2 teaspoons minced garlic

½ teaspoon cayenne pepper

½ teaspoon chili powder

½ teaspoon Cajun seasoning

Dash hot sauce

Salt and pepper to taste

Brown ground beef and drain grease, reserving a tablespoon in skillet to sauté chopped onion. When onion is translucent, place in large soup pot and add drained beans along with chopped green chilies and stewed tomatoes. Stir in beef broth, garlic, and seasonings. Heat to boiling, reduce heat, and simmer for 30 to 45 minutes.

Worries go down better with soup.

JEWISH PROVERB

I'm curious—how many times will you ask people to repeat themselves before you smile and act like you understand—even if you still don't have a clue? Three used to be my limit. I have since reconsidered that practice. The following story may encourage you to, as well.

Mama and I had traveled to Texas to visit my daughter and her family. While there, we took Mama out to eat at a well-known Mexican restaurant for her birthday. Early in our meal, I snuck off to ask our waiter if they could sing "Happy Birthday" to my mother. I was thinking of something like, "Happy, happy birthday, we're so glad you came—"

"Sí," the waiter said in response to my request, "but we must garble, garble, garble. Eet's tradeetional."

"Excuse me?" I asked.

"We must garble, garble," he said. "Eet's tradeetional."

I tried again, but after the third garble, I smiled brightly. "Okay, sounds great!" Surely one can't blame the man for assuming we had an agreement.

Shortly afterward, some merry waiters came singing out of the kitchen, clear across the restaurant. I watched, in horror, as they smashed a cream pie into a birthday stranger's face. Meanwhile, my own dear mama sat across the table from me, playing with her great-grandson, blissfully unaware of the impending doom! At that very moment, a second band of evil servers began approaching our table with Mama's pie.

No!!!

I panicked. It was like a slow motion dream. I couldn't breathe, I couldn't speak—I waved my arms wildly and sputtered incoherently. *Sweet Jesus, so this was garble, garble!*

I'll never know if it was the terror on my face or if he was overcome by mercy because I was calling on the good Lord, but at the last moment the lead waiter smeared a dab of whipped cream on Mama's nose with his finger, which she took with great class. I, meanwhile, was left signaling for oxygen.

The moral of my story and my helpful PSA: if at first you don't understand, you may want to ask until you do.

Strange how much you've got to know
before you know how little you know.

UNKNOWN

Multi-Herb Gremolata Butter from Kitchen Belleicious

Gremolata butter is music to my ears. You may have heard of it, but chances are you haven't made it because you probably never realized how many uses it has and how easy it is to prepare. I mean, if you knew how amazingly simple it is to make and how useful it is, you would be in the kitchen right now churning up some butter, right? Right! Well, let's go!

¾ cup (1½ sticks) butter, room temperature

⅓ cup plus 2 tablespoons chopped herbs: parsley, thyme, oregano, sage, and basil

¾ teaspoon salt

¾ teaspoon pepper

1 tablespoon lemon zest plus 1 tablespoon juice

3 teaspoons minced shallots

In stand mixer bowl fitted with paddle attachment and/or a large bowl using a spatula, combine all ingredients. Spoon butter onto parchment or plastic wrap and roll into log. Store in refrigerator for up to 2 to 3 days, or for best results freeze butter log in foil and slice as needed.

Penny's Killer Guacamole

I'm pretty much a Johnny-come-lately to the avocado-based delight of guacamole, but I came around in a big way when my friend Penny whipped up her guacamole on a girls' trip to Florida a couple of summers ago. Here's the recipe that did it!

6 avocados

Juice of 2 limes

½ teaspoon chopped garlic

½ teaspoon cilantro

2 small chopped tomatoes (or 1 can drained RoTel)

Fresh chopped jalapeños to taste

Salt and pepper to taste

Peel avocados and remove seeds. Mash avocado flesh in mixing bowl with juice of 2 limes. I leave mine sort of chunky, but you can make it as smooth as you'd like.

Season with minced garlic and cilantro. Stir in chopped tomatoes and fresh chopped jalapeños. You can adjust jalapeños to your family's liking. We like things hot, so I use about 2 to 4, depending on their size. Stir well, salt and pepper to taste, and transfer to serving bowl. Perfection.

Hugo's Famous Salad Dressing

Hugo was a fine Italian gentleman who used to run a restaurant in our hometown, Lake Providence, Louisiana. Hugo's salad had a reputation all its own, and it was all due to his famous salad dressing. How my late mother-in-law got the secret out of Hugo is anybody's guess, but that's another story.

3 ounces garlic oil

3 ounces apple cider vinegar

2 tablespoons capers

1 tablespoon crushed oregano

1 tablespoon crushed black pepper

½ tablespoon salt

Combine garlic oil and vinegar in glass jar with tight lid. Shake well to mix. Add capers, crushed oregano, black pepper, and salt. Mix well.

Drizzle generously over fresh lettuce. Top with green and black olives and a cubed tomato.

Belle Tip:

You simply must use garlic oil to get the flavor right in this dressing. If you can't find garlic oil on your grocery shelf, I'd recommend adding several minced garlic cloves to a jar of olive oil and allowing it to marinate for a few days!

Shellie's Super Spaghetti Sauce

I'm happy to share my homemade spaghetti sauce with y'all. I think it's good, mamma mia good, but then I've gotten to where I don't like to use anything processed if I can help it. It's better for your taste buds and your insides.

2 cups diced onion, pepper, celery blend, frozen or fresh

2 tablespoons butter

1 to 2 pounds ground beef

1 tablespoon olive oil

2 cloves minced garlic

2 (28 ounce) cans crushed tomatoes

2 tablespoons dried basil

1 tablespoon sugar

2 teaspoons pepper

1 teaspoon oregano

1 teaspoon thyme

1 teaspoon parsley

¼ cup grated Romano cheese

Sauté onion, pepper, celery blend in butter in skillet. Remove veggies and use skillet to brown ground beef. Drain beef and return to skillet. In large saucepan, heat olive oil and minced garlic. Stir 1 to 2 minutes to develop flavor, but be careful that your garlic doesn't burn. Add sauce, seasonings, and sautéed veggies to skillet with browned and drained beef. Heat to boiling, reduce to medium heat, and cook at least 1 hour.

The longer this cooks, the deeper the flavor gets. (I say that, but in the interest of full disclosure, I rarely start my sauce as soon as I should to let that happen.) In the last 30 minutes, I like to drop in about ¼ cup grated Romano cheese. It adds a nice kick. Serve over your favorite spaghetti or vermicelli noodles topped with grated parmesan.

Basic White Sauce

Every home cook needs to know how to whip up a basic white sauce. Make an alfredo out of this roux by adding heavy cream and grated parmesan cheese. Add sliced mushrooms when a recipe calls for mushroom soup, chicken broth when you need chicken soup, etc. You can even experiment with different cheeses and herbs. For instance, I use thyme and garlic for my alfredo, and I spice up my white sauce with Cajun seasoning when I'm serving it over a blackened chicken or seafood dish.

2 to 3 tablespoons butter

2 to 3 tablespoons flour

1 cup milk

Melt 2 to 3 tablespoons butter in skillet over medium heat. Stir in 2 to 3 tablespoons flour. Slowly stir in 1 cup milk until it's incorporated and let it simmer.

Homemade BBQ Sauce from Kitchen Belleicious

Say no more to store-bought sauce. This homemade version is easy and quick. It is bone-suckin', gotta-have-it-now kind of good, and you can't go wrong with it! Best of all, the sauce base is versatile and lends itself to whatever way you want to take it. More mustard? Yes, please. More vinegar? Why not? A touch of red pepper flakes or adobe sauce can bring the heat! Be creative! And make an extra batch to freeze for a rainy day—or, rather, a sunny day.

1¼ cups ketchup

⅛ cup Saucy Mama yellow mustard

⅓ cup distilled apple cider vinegar

4 tablespoons Worcestershire sauce

¾ cup brown sugar

¼ cup cane syrup

2½ tablespoons butter

2 teaspoons balsamic vinegar

2 teaspoons garlic powder

1 teaspoon onion powder

1 teaspoon chili powder

1 teaspoon ancho chili powder

½ teaspoon fine sea salt

½ teaspoon black pepper

Combine all ingredients in medium saucepan. Heat to boiling, then reduce heat and simmer for 5 minutes or until sugar has dissolved. Allow mixture to simmer until thickened to your preference. Serve warm or cover tightly in plastic or glass container and store in fridge.

Cheesy Vegetable Soup

Yes, this soup has a pound of Velveeta in it, which means it isn't exactly light in calories. That's okay—it's not light in flavor either, but you'll find it's worth the indulgence.

6 medium potatoes, diced

3 to 4 onions, diced

5 cups water

1 (16 ounce) bag frozen mixed vegetables

1 cup shredded carrots

1 tablespoon butter

3 tablespoons flour

½ cup chicken broth

½ cup milk

1 pound Velveeta, cubed

1 pound fresh mushrooms, sliced

1 clove minced garlic

Salt and pepper to taste

1 bay leaf

Clean and dice potatoes and onions. Add to 5 cups boiling water. As soon as potatoes are "fork tender," add frozen mixed vegetables and shredded carrots. Stir until soup comes back to a boil. Reduce heat to low and simmer while you stir up a simple white sauce.

In small saucepan, melt 1 tablespoon butter and whisk in 2 to 3 tablespoons flour. Once smooth, remove from heat and whisk in chicken broth and milk. Heat to boiling, stirring continuously until it thickens.

Add white sauce to fork-tender veggies, stir, and add cubed Velveeta. Fold in sliced mushrooms and minced garlic. Season to taste with salt and pepper, add bay leaf, and cook on low about 30 minutes.

My All Things Southern Comeback Sauce

Comeback sauce is a highly favored southern condiment that is crazy versatile. You can dress salads or pastas with it or use it as a dip for seafood and french fries. However you try it, you'll come back for more, which is exactly how it got its name. Most every southern cook or restaurant has their own version of this southern condiment, and while they all begin with a similar base, the recipe is wide open after that. Here's My All Things Southern Comeback Sauce.

1 cup mayonnaise

1 cup ketchup

1 cup vegetable oil

1 lemon, juiced

Dash hot sauce

1 clove garlic, minced

1 teaspoon prepared mustard

1 teaspoon pepper

1 teaspoon paprika

1 teaspoon Worcestershire sauce

½ teaspoon horseradish

1 small onion, minced and sautéed

Salt to taste

In mixing bowl, build base by combining mayonnaise, ketchup, and oil. Add juice of 1 lemon, hot sauce, minced garlic, mustard, pepper, paprika, and Worcestershire, and—here's one of my favorite twists—horseradish. That'll kick it up.

Here's another secret. Most people use raw onion. I like to mince a small white onion and sauté it in a tablespoon of butter before adding it to my sauce. Comeback sauce will keep in the refrigerator if you put it in an airtight container.

CRANKED UP CRANBERRY RELISH

*I've never been a fan of the molded cranberry, but this past Thanksgiving
I was pressured into whipping up a cranberry relish of my very own!
Blame it on Sandra Lee, Bobby, Giada, and the rest of 'em. Yep, I was watching
the Food Network again, and I had to try my hand at my very own cranberry
relish. I took a few ideas from this one and a couple from that one—voilà! It
was a huge hit at our house. We found it to be delicious with the turkey and
rolls, and I'm thinking it would even be tasty with chips! I'm always on the
lookout for a new dip, you know. Come on, folks, let's get started!*

2 cups canned cranberries
(not molded)

¼ cup chopped green bell
pepper

3 jalapeño peppers, seeded
and chopped

¼ cup chopped white onion

¼ cup chopped green onion

½ cup chopped cilantro

¼ cup lime juice

¾ cup sugar

½ teaspoon cumin

¼ teaspoon salt

Break down fresh cranberries in food processor.
Combine with bell pepper, jalapeños, and white and
green onions. Season with cilantro, lime juice, sugar,
cumin, and salt. Chill for at least 30 minutes before
serving!

> *The nice thing about southerners is the way we enjoy our neuroses.*
> FLORENCE KING

⟐━•━•━•━•━•━•━•━•━•━•━•━•━•━•━•━•━•━•━•━⟐

*S*hortly after the release of my second humor book, *Sue Ellen's Girl Ain't Fat, She Just Weighs Heavy!* I launched an organization to combat a syndrome I had officially researched, documented, and christened straight running crazy, or SRC for short. Someone with SRC is no longer detouring from more lucid behavior but going full-steam ahead.

The current rate of infection even moved me to create an SRC Facebook group so I could ask my readers to alert me to straight running crazy outbreaks wherever they find them. It's proven difficult to even keep up with that page due to the increasing proliferation of SRC sightings, let alone promote it. Please consider joining that Facebook group. Frankly, it's going to take all of us to get the word out.

Our motto is "Commit yourself to raising awareness of SRC," and my first official SRC documentation was to address mantie-wearing menfolk. Yes, there's a story here.

I really enjoy sharing group text messages with my immediate family. With a cell phone on every hip, it's a cool way to have group conversations at the drop of a hat, and everyone usually replies quickly. There have been certain exceptions.

One day I messaged the menfolk concerning what I was thinking about getting them for Christmas that year—manties—and then I waited eagerly for a response.

I got nothing.

It was so quiet my text was echoing. Not one word from Phil, Patrick, or Phillip. I couldn't even get my guys to talk about manties. That would be man panties, the big thing in high fashion—according to my Internet research.

I explained to my men that I could order their manties in high-cuts or briefs, with or without lace, and for a few extra dollars, I could even have 'em embroidered with their names. Again, they missed the humor completely. And seriously, dear ones, that is A-OK with this belle.

By the way, my friend Paulette thinks this topic could get me a ton of negative publicity, but I feel duty bound to call it the way I see it for the good of all mankind. Should any of the men fashionistas take issue with me, I will politely suggest that they heed the advice that has served my fellow belles and me so well for so long, "Put on your big boy manties and deal with it."

I've been known to opine on some straight running crazy developments just so I can quit thinking about the nonsense coming at me from every direction, like baby wigs. You can now buy hairpieces for your baby on the Internet. Yes, you can.

To be perfectly clear, I'm not talking about helping children who are losing their hair in a serious health battle. I'm talking about mothers who are so uncomfortable with their female babies' little bald heads that they're willing to dress the poor things up in tiny headbands with attached fake bangs.

I couldn't make this up if I tried. Someone has serious hair issues here, and it's not the wee one. For the record, I feel like I've earned the right to opine mother-daughter hair issues. I have some serious experience here, albeit on an entirely different level.

My daughter has given me permission to tell y'all her preteen fixation with hair bumps. Hopefully, I won't have nightmares later from dredging up these memories, but here we go.

We went through a season around our house when preteen Jessica found it impossible to put her hair in a ponytail and leave it alone if she found the slightest bump on the top of her head. There was no reasoning with Jessica Ann on the bump issue. If her hair wasn't melted butter smooth, she'd jerk that ponytail out and start over and over and over again. At the time, I was also serving as Jessica's extremely intense basketball coach. I once found my entire team on the floor warming up for the game, while my own sweet daughter was still in the dressing room battling those dreaded bumps. Let's just say a notorious hair battle ensued.

Frankly, I think infant hairpieces are straight running crazy, but I'm willing to admit something: had there been a preteen hairpiece option in Jessica's bump years, I may have walked on the wild side myself.

Hungry is a mighty fine sauce.
SOUTHERN SAYING

Perfect Pea Topping Relish

This scrumptious relish can top those fresh peas you've been hankering for, or it can be served as a delicious low-calorie dip. Pair it with some baked chips and congratulate yourself for skipping the Ro-Tel and cheese dip—at least today. But remember, don't deny yourself too long, honey—
you'll just fall off the wagon in the end.

1 (4 ounce) can chopped green chilies

1 (2.25 ounce) can chopped ripe olives

1 (10 ounce) can Ro-Tel tomatoes

1 bunch green onions, chopped

2 tablespoons extra virgin olive oil

1 teaspoon vinegar

1 teaspoon garlic powder

1 teaspoon Cajun seasoning

Salt and pepper to taste

Combine green chilies, olives, tomatoes, and green onions. Add extra virgin olive oil, vinegar, garlic powder, Cajun seasoning, and salt and pepper to taste. Chill while peas are cooking. Enjoy!

And finally, at least for the sake of this chapter, longtime listeners of my radio show are familiar with another version of SRC that gets my attention faster than quick. Simply put, when nekked news breaks out, I break in. This is mostly because the word *nekked* makes me laugh, but also because I remain fascinated by what makes people want to take their clothes off in public. When nekked news breaks out anywhere on the globe, I aim to cover it. Pun intended.

The most recent nekked story to catch my attention concerned my interest in learning that, should you have a hankering to stand nekked in the open doorway of your own home, you may do so—at least in Charlotte, North Carolina, where one resident has been proving this theory several times a week for the last decade. According to officials, Nekked Man is within his rights because he is technically exposing himself in the privacy of his own home and not in the public square.

Nekked Man's neighbors are not happy with that verdict. They continue to lodge their complaints with the authorities, who are looking into other ways to address the issue. I particularly enjoyed how one neighbor expressed her frustration to the local television station, and I'm quoting here: "I was rolling out the trash can Friday morning and I just happened to look over, and there he was, buck naked."

I realize some will question whether he was, in fact, butt nekked or buck nekked, but I don't have time for that age-old debate. I'm on a different mission.

Because of my well-documented history of opining on nekked news, it might surprise people to know that I've come to use similar phrasing during my prayer times. It's true. In recent years, I've become increasingly grateful to the Lord for stripping me down spiritually and giving me a nekked faith. I tell Him so on a regular basis.

I'm full of prayers, passion, and good intentions, but I no longer trust any of those things to enjoy the abiding friendship of God provided me in Christ Jesus. I now have a nekked faith in God's Son, and I'm always asking the Father to remind me anytime I try and find confidence in my confessions or in my self-efforts to please Him. I stand in the doorway that is Christ the Lord, meeting place between God and man, and it is a perfect rest.

HOMEMADE WHIPPED CREAM

*Here's another recipe rescue. Why run to the store for that carton of
Cool Whip when you can make a tastier, fresher version in no time flat!*

2 tablespoons powdered
  sugar
1 cup heavy cream
1 teaspoon vanilla

Combine ingredients and beat until peaks form!
Remember, if you put your mixing bowl in the freezer
a few minutes before you prepare, it will whip up faster
and stiffer!

AUNT ELAINE'S HOT FUDGE SAUCE

*You can use this hot fudge topping as a complement to
various desserts, over ice cream, or as a dip for fresh fruit.*

¾ cup cocoa
1 cup sugar
¾ teaspoon salt
1 teaspoon vanilla
½ cup evaporated milk
1 cup light corn syrup
2 tablespoons butter

Stir together first 3 ingredients. Add remaining
ingredients. Microwave on high 3 minutes. Enjoy!

6

APPETIZERS TO TAKE THE EDGE OFF

THOUGHTS ON LOVE AND WAR

Where there is strife, there is pride.
PROVERBS 13:10 NIV

I had to wait a good long while to tell this story, but ever since I got clearance from the parties involved, I've been busy telling it here, there, and yonder. It's just too good. I even put it in my storytelling CD, *Y'all Asked for It*, a work of love so titled because folks had been asking me for audio recordings of my stories at my product table. I can work this tale into most any speech, given a minute or two to come up with a clever segue, but it's a perfect opening for a chapter on love and war. (See how I did that? We professional storytellers know these tricks.)

When this first happened to my friend Caroline—and that is absolutely a fake name—Caroline had a hard time finding the funny in it. "You aren't allowed to tell this on the radio," she said. "Promise me!" I did promise, and though it tried my soul, I didn't tell.

Then one day Caroline called about a recipe, and I brought the story back up, sort of testing the water to see if it was still off-limits. "Oh, please," she

said. "My man has told everyone this side of the Mississippi; you might as well share it with your readers and give everyone a laugh." So, with her blessing, we'll proceed.

Many moons ago, Caroline found herself half awake in the middle of the night, aware that she needed to use the restroom but not wanting to wake up for fear she wouldn't be able to fall back asleep. So, without opening her eyes, Caroline got out of bed and began feeling her way to the bathroom with her hands—hoping to stay in that dreamlike state.

This may have worked for my friend; we'll never know. For unknown to the sleepwalking Caroline, her dearly beloved had felt a similar nighttime urge. He was sitting quietly on the very spot his wife was headed toward and fate was presenting him with a marvelous opportunity: his sweetie was approaching him in the dead of night with her eyes closed.

Just as sweet Caroline lowered her

pajama bottoms and sat down, her man wrapped his big old arms around her midsection and squeezed. Faster than you can say "justifiable homicide," the poor girl was wide awake. And what's more, now she and her man needed a shower!

Caroline told me that she remembered backing up against the wall and continuing to scream long after she realized she was safe and she wasn't being attacked by a toilet bugger. My favorite part of this story, however, is what she said next.

"I want you to know," Caroline deadpanned drily, "my man hasn't felt safe a day since." Let she who would not want to harm him cast the first stone. Amen.

Super-Duper Dixie Quesadillas

Whether they're for a band of kids looking for an after-school snack or a group of fans fresh from cheering on their favorite sports team, my Super-Duper Dixie Quesadillas can be whipped up in no time flat and served as an appetizer to whatever hungry crowd has found their way to your place.

2 (10 inch) flour tortillas

¾ cup chunky salsa

1 (4 ounce) can green chilies, drained and diced

½ cup sliced black olives

1 cup grated Monterey Jack cheese

Place tortillas on ungreased baking sheet and spread to edges with a tablespoon or so of your favorite chunky salsa. Combine green chilies with sliced black olives and sprinkle over salsa before topping with shredded Monterey Jack. Bake at 425 degrees for 10 minutes or until tortillas are crisp and cheese is melted. Use pizza cutter to slice each tortilla into 8 wedges and you've got 16 delicious appetizers. Just repeat the process for a crowd. You'll be the "toast" of the party!

Belle Tip:

Try the Green Tomatillo Salsa Verde from Kitchen Belleicious on page 164 in this recipe!

Keep 'Em Coming Smokies

Here's a great party recipe you can throw in the slow cooker and forget about while you're tending to the other hundred dozen details!

3 (14 ounce) packages little smokies

1 (16 ounce) can whole berry cranberry sauce

½ cup ketchup

½ cup pure maple syrup

1 tablespoon Spicy Brown Grey Poupon mustard

1 (18 ounce) bottle barbecue sauce

Place little smokies in slow cooker. Blend cranberry sauce with ketchup, maple syrup, and mustard in small bowl. Stir in barbecue sauce. Pour mixture over little smokies, set slow cooker to low, and walk away. They'll be ready when you are!

Lamar's Man-Sized Snacks

Around our house, our favored methods of using all that venison meat in the freezer is to smother and quick fry it or cook it up in big batches of chili. At least, it was. That is, until our good friends had Phil and me over for supper and Lamar served us these man-sized appetizers while the main course was cooking. The good news is that Lamar was willing to share his secrets.

Venison steaks

Tony Chachere's Original Creole Seasoning

Garlic salt

Pepper

Panola Spicy Sweet Jalapeño Peppers (you can find 'em on the Internet)

Peppered bacon

Season steaks well with creole seasoning, garlic salt, and pepper. Place 3 or 4 jalapeño peppers in center of each steak, roll up, and wrap with half slice of peppered bacon. If you don't use peppered bacon, at least make sure you use a heavy bacon—none of that flimsy see-through stuff. Cook 20 to 30 minutes on grill over low flame and enjoy!

Belle Tip:

You can also make your own sweet and spicy peppers. Just drain a jar of jalapeño slices and add a cup of sugar. Recap, shake, and refrigerate for several days, turning over occasionally.

*S*ometimes our interpersonal relationships are challenged by our evolving English language. Whether we like it or not, definitions change over the years. I'm a word person. I get that. I've been trying to explain it to my darling man. Phil's having a bit more trouble, and in some ways, it's getting Phil into a bit more trouble.

Exhibit A: We were watching one of the singing competition shows the other night. My man and I freely admit that neither of us can sing, and we aren't the best judges of musical talent. That said, we still like to watch the process of new talent being discovered and developed. That particular night one of the contestants had just done what we both thought was a fine job crooning a good old country hit.

"He's good," Phil said.

No sooner did my man get that out of his mouth than the song ended and the camera turned to one of the celebrity judges, who looked at the budding singer and said, "That was sick."

Phil looked at me as if to say, "Did you hear him? How rude."

"That means he's good," I told Phil. "*Sick* means good these days."

My darling rolled his eyes, and we went back to watching the program. A few minutes later one of the judges told a contestant right to her face that she was bad.

Phil looked back at me. "Good," I said. "Bad means good, too."

I got zero response that time.

Several days later I was all dressed up and headed out of town. Phil was in the kitchen going through the mail when I walked through and commented that I didn't feel so good. My sweet man looked up and smiled. "Well," he said, "you look sick."

"Excuse me?"

"You know what I mean," Phil said. "You look bad."

"Excuse me?" I repeated. I finally realized what was happening when Phil sighed deeply and asked, "Just tell me. How many tries do I have left?"

You don't have to attend every argument you're invited to.
Unknown

$\mathcal{P}$hil's honest confusion puts me in mind of another great story about the challenges of communication. I hope you'll enjoy it half as much as I do. Oh, and for the record, I'll be cleaning up the dialogue just a tad bit by substituting a southern expression I learned from my own dear mama.

Meet Mr. Wallace. He's a good friend of our family and a really funny fellow who is loved by everyone who has the privilege of knowing him. Mr. Wallace turned eighty-five awhile back, but he's still going strong, and he continues to light up a room with his great big personality.

One day Mr. Wallace and his sweet wife had gone to our local country club for lunch. And, as is his custom, Mr. Wallace had greeted everyone in the club before he and Mrs. Wanda finally took a table beside a young man named Captain Jack Junior. Mr. Wallace could remember when Jack was born. It was during the ensuing conversation that Mr. Wallace noticed young Jack was wearing a handsome new watch with a beautiful gold face.

"I like that watch, Jack," Mr. Wallace said. "What is it?"

"Guess," Jack replied.

That answer didn't set so well with Mr. Wallace, who didn't realize Jack was referring to the brand. His reply has been fondly recounted in these parts ever since.

"H–e–double l, Jack," Mr. Wallace said. "If I had wanted to guess, I wouldn't have asked you!"

Fall's Favorite Spice Tea

We southerners have learned to be flexible about what constitutes a new season. If the calendar says it's fall, by golly, it's fall! Long before our stubborn trees give up a leaf and regardless of whether we need shorts or sweaters, we take our make-the-best-of-it upbringing and deem that the season has arrived. We'll pull out our pumpkin recipes and seasonal decorations to the hum of the air conditioner. At this house, the first ode to fall begins with the Making of the Tea, a tradition traced back to my mama's house. Everything about it feeds my soul—from the colors to the smells to the memories of countless cups shared with family and friends.

1 cup instant tea

2 cups lemonade mix

2 cups Tang instant breakfast drink

1 cup sugar (optional)

1 teaspoon ground cinnamon

1 teaspoon ground cloves

1 teaspoon allspice

Mix all ingredients and store in closed container. For a great cup of spice tea, heat a mug full of water and stir in 2 to 3 heaping teaspoons, depending on how strong you like it. Believe it or not, back in the day I would use 2 full cups of sugar in this recipe. These days I either use half the amount of sugar or leave it out completely! I think there's plenty of sweetness in the Tang and lemonade mix. You can always add a teaspoon to your cup if you need it sweeter. Or stick your finger in it if you're really sweet.

Belle Tip:

For a wassail flavor, substitute orange juice for the water!

Yeah, the appetizer, that's the food we eat before we have our food. . . . No, you're thinking of dessert, that's the food we eat after we have our food.

Jim Gaffigan

Barbecued Pecans

*My Barbecued Pecans are great munchies for after-school snacks,
sports parties, or your personal coffee break. The hot sauce is going
to kick up the heat, so do adjust it to your family's tastes.*

2 tablespoons butter

1 tablespoon ketchup

¼ cup Worcestershire sauce

2 dashes hot sauce

4 cups pecan halves

Melt butter in small saucepan. Stir in ketchup,
Worcestershire sauce, and hot sauce. Pour over pecan
halves, stir to coat, and spread evenly in 9x13 baking
pan. Roast at 400 degrees for 20 minutes, but watch
'em carefully so they don't burn. Drain on paper towels
and enjoy!

Crazy Good Artichoke Bruschetta

Bruschetta is a starter dish that begins with grilled bread (basically toast). This recipe utilizes marinated artichokes and kalamata olives to bring big-time flavor!

1 baguette, sliced into ½-inch thick servings

1 tablespoon olive oil

1 (7.5 ounce) jar marinated artichoke hearts, drained and chopped

1 (2 ounce) jar diced pimientos, drained

⅓ cup chopped and pitted kalamata olives

½ cup chives and onion cream cheese

Preheat oven to 400 degrees. Brush one side of baguette with olive oil. Place it oil side down on ungreased cookie sheet and toast it for 4 to 5 minutes.

Meanwhile, in mixing bowl combine artichoke hearts, pimientos, olives, and cream cheese. Turn toasted bread over and spread with artichoke mixture. Return to oven for 3 to 5 minutes or until cheese is melted.

Green Tomatillo Salsa Verde from Kitchen Belleicious

This authentic salsa verde has an amazing fresh flavor that you won't find in any store-bought version. You can use this salsa on just about anything from meat to seafood, but I like it best with a big bowl of chips.

1 pound fresh tomatillos, peeled and cleaned

1 small onion, quartered

4 cloves garlic, whole

Olive oil

Sea salt

1 teaspoon each salt and pepper

1 teaspoon red pepper flakes

½ cup packed cilantro

Splash red wine vinegar

Juice of 1 lime

1 teaspoon jalapeño juice or ½ jalapeño, minced

Place whole tomatillos, quartered onions, and whole garlic cloves on baking sheet drizzled with olive oil and sprinkled with sea salt. Roast at 400 degrees for 15 minutes or until slightly browned with charred appearance. Note: make sure garlic cloves are well drizzled with olive oil or they will burn.

Place all ingredients in food processor or blender and blend until slightly smooth. (I personally prefer a little texture with my salsa.)

CHRISTMAS SNACKIN' CRACKERS

One of the Tomlinson family's holiday favorites is Christmas Snackin' Crackers! This recipe takes regular old saltine crackers and turns them into a holiday favorite. Warning: making 'em is simple—keeping 'em hid from the family long enough to soak up the seasonings is where the real challenge lies!

2 cups canola oil
1 package ranch dressing mix
1 tablespoon red pepper
1 tablespoon garlic powder
1 box saltine crackers

Combine canola oil with ranch dressing mix, red pepper, and garlic powder. Stir well and pour over entire box of saltine crackers in large plastic bowl. Using your hands or a large spoon, turn crackers several times to coat. Cover bowl with tight lid and turn occasionally while crackers are absorbing seasoned oil. Crackers can be marinated in plastic bag instead of bowl, but be careful not to break crackers.

Snackin' Crackers take a day to a day and a half to soak up seasonings, but they are definitely worth the wait. Crackers are ready when all oil is absorbed.

All-Fired-Up Cheese Krispies

*Most every southern cook has a favorite cheese straw recipe.
Mine incorporates crisp rice cereal for some serious crunch. These keep
well in a cookie tin. Be the hostess with the mostest and share 'em
with your drop-in guests along with a hot cup of coffee!*

1 cup (2 sticks) butter, softened

½ pound sharp cheddar cheese, grated

2 cups self-rising flour

1 teaspoon garlic powder

Dash each salt and pepper

Dash red pepper

Dash hot sauce

2 cups crisp rice cereal

Preheat oven to 350 degrees. Mix butter with grated sharp cheddar and self-rising flour. Add garlic powder, salt, pepper, red pepper, and hot sauce. Stir in cereal. Roll rounded tablespoonfuls of dough into balls. Flatten balls on ungreased cookie sheet and make criss-cross design on tops with fork. Bake 15 minutes.

Why must I love cheese. . .and bread. . .and cheesy bread?
UNKNOWN

*H*ere's some insider information on my work here: my readers write a lot of my material. (Don't tell my publishers! It's a great gig—if you can get it going! That's the hard part.)

Seriously, my readers tell me stories that are every bit as good as, and usually better than, mine! One of my book tour stops left me with a load of great stories and a new heroine, a mature belle named Poncy.

Poncy has gone to her eternal reward, but her legend lives on. I was introduced to Poncy via her adorable granddaughter Brocky. (Cute nicknames seem to be a family thing. Poncy's given name was Mary Florence, but Poncy was the best her little brother could do with such a mouthful.) Poncy was an Alabama belle of the highest order, the type of genteel southern matriarch who oozed class without trying. One of my favorite Poncy stories—and Brocky had several—happened years ago at an Ole Miss versus Auburn football game.

Poncy and her husband, G.L., a proud Auburn grad, had the misfortune that day to be seated in front of the Ole Miss student section. They weren't pleased, but they were making the best of a bad situation, right up until The Incident. That would be when one of the Auburn players got hurt. Poncy sat in concerned silence as four men and a gurney came onto the field to tote the poor guy away. Not everyone followed her lead. As frat boys will do, the Ole Miss guys started chanting in unison, "Don't carry him! Bury him! Don't carry him! Bury him!"

Poncy was appalled at their behavior. And by the third or fourth chant, she could no longer restrain herself. Standing and turning to face the unruly college crowd, she raised her voice several octaves and made a loud announcement to the hecklers in a staccato style accompanied with a defiant glare, "That–is–my–son!"

Having effectively quieted the rowdy crowd, Poncy took her seat to find G.L. looking at her over the rim of his glasses. "Mary Florence," he scolded.

Poncy was undeterred. "Well," she said matter-of-factly, "he's somebody's son!"

Here, here, Poncy!

•─◦═◦═◦═◦═◦═◦═◦═◦═◦═◦═◦═◦─•

Do the right thing. It will gratify
some people and astonish the rest.

MARK TWAIN

$\mathcal{P}$oor old Jerry Reed could've benefited from having a Poncy in his corner back in the day. But I haven't introduced y'all to Brother Jerry, have I? I'm sorry. Let's fix that.

Many years ago, my Papaw, the Reverend Marvin Stone, acted as a mentor to another young pastor named Brother Jerry Reed. Papaw Stone was a full-time preacher with a flair for comedy. He was a great help to Brother Jerry on the ministry end, but bless his heart, his mentee had to put up with a lot of Papaw's shenanigans.

In the early days of Brother Jerry's ministry, Papaw let Brother Jerry get his feet wet by preaching for Papaw on Sunday nights at Riverside Baptist Church. One Sunday morning, Papaw asked Brother Jerry what he'd be preaching on that evening.

"Snake handling," Brother Jerry announced. Say what?

As Brother Jerry went on to explain, he intended to grab the congregation's attention with the subject matter so he could preach on how to handle the snake of jealousy, the snake of gossip, and so forth. That explanation was enough for Papaw.

That evening as the congregation reconvened, circumstances presented Papaw with an opportunity the prankster in him simply couldn't resist. Upon his arrival, one of the deacons mentioned to Papaw that he had run over the biggest, blackest snake he had ever seen in the parking lot out front. Oh, really? Papaw happened to know that Brother Jerry had placed a paper bag beside the pulpit. In it was a five-foot-long rubber snake Brother Jerry intended to use for illustration. Yes, my papaw did. When Brother Jerry wasn't looking, Papaw switched that fake rubber snake for the very real but freshly dead one.

Sometime later Brother Jerry was preaching hard and heavy about old Slew Foot and the snakes that trip up the unsuspecting, when he became Exhibit A. As he reached the big moment in his sermon, Brother Jerry stuck his hand in that bag intending to pull out a fake plastic snake. He came out with a warm, scaly real one instead.

Papaw liked to say that Brother Jerry was in a hurry to let go of that snake.

With a holler, Brother Jerry threw that varmint over his head, over the choir loft, and into the baptistery. The snake's flight path took it directly over the choir members, who promptly split down the middle like the Red Sea and exited in record speed.

That's what you call a big finish.

I don't know if anybody got right that night at Riverside Baptist Church, but I think we all know who needed to! Can I get a witness? Seems an excellent place to celebrate the glorious truth:

The ground is level at the cross. Won't you kneel with me?

Papaw has been gone for many a year, but Mama and Aunt Marleta got to visit with Brother Jerry Reed recently. They couldn't help but reminisce about all the old stories, and in doing so, they had to ask him about his sinuses for old times' sake. Brother Jerry said he hadn't had a problem with his sinuses since their daddy fixed him up! Oh yeah, there's a story there.

It happened one day that Brother Jerry was at Papaw's house when he began to complain about his sinuses. Papaw told him to sit tight, that he had just the thing—and off he went to the medicine chest to retrieve some highly effective nose drops that he himself had used months before. Only Papaw had forgotten that he'd used up all of those nose drops and refilled the bottle with his old coon dog's mange medicine. We're talking full-strength turpentine.

Papaw instructed Brother Jerry to lay his head back on the chair. Then he took the eye dropper and filled it up with what both men thought was super-duper clean-your-sinuses-out nose spray. They were not disappointed.

Papaw filled both of Brother Jerry's nostrils before his poor friend could even react, but a couple of seconds later, the pain-paralyzed Brother Jerry saw the light. He shot off that chair and commenced to hollering, jumping, and running circles around the house.

How fast was he? Well, Papaw used to say Brother Jerry was running so fast he thought he was gonna have to snort some of that stuff up his own nose just to catch him!

Monterey Jack and Green Chilies Dip

My family can get straight running crazy about basketball. It's become something of a tradition around our place for me to come up with new dips to celebrate the college play-offs known as March Madness. My Monterey Jack and Green Chiles Dip topped the charts several years back. It's a delicious white dip reminiscent of queso that will make you think you're dining at your favorite Mexican restaurant.

1 medium onion, chopped

2 tablespoons vegetable oil

2 (4.5 ounce) cans diced green chilies

½ teaspoon salt

1 (5 ounce) can evaporated milk

1 cup grated Monterey Jack cheese

Sauté onion in vegetable oil until clear. Add green chilies and salt. Slowly stir in evaporated milk and cook 5 minutes. When mixture begins to thicken, add Monterey Jack. Mix in blender for a really smooth sauce. Serve warm with your favorite chips or veggies. Good luck to your team! (Unless they're playing ours.)

Hot Crabmeat Dip

This dip is best with fresh crabmeat, but I've been known to substitute an 8-ounce package of Louis Kemp Crab Delights Imitation Flake Style Crab Meat in a pinch. It's not as soft and sweet as the real seafood, but it will still produce a tasty dip!

8 ounces cream cheese, softened

2 tablespoons milk

2 tablespoons minced onion

1 teaspoon prepared horseradish

¼ teaspoon salt

Pinch pepper

1 (6 ounce) can crabmeat, drained and flaked

⅓ cup sliced almonds

Preheat oven to 350 degrees. Mix cream cheese, milk, onion, horseradish, salt, pepper, and crabmeat. Spread mixture into pie pan or shallow baking dish. Sprinkle almonds across top and bake 45 minutes or until bubbly and lightly browned.

All-Cheesed-Up Artichoke Dip

My family loves artichoke dips, but none of us are fond of the ones that use a strong mayonnaise base. I developed this recipe around our favorite cheeses, limited the mayo, hit it with a dash of hot pepper, and created a winner in our book!

8 ounces cream cheese

½ cup mayonnaise

14 ounces marinated artichoke hearts

3 green onions, diced

1 cup grated Monterey Jack cheese

1 (5 ounce) package Frigo 3-Cheese Italian Blend (grated Parmesan, Asiago, and Romano)

Dash hot sauce

Salt and pepper

Preheat oven to 350 degrees. Blend cream cheese and mayonnaise in food processor. Add marinated artichoke hearts, green onions, and remaining cheeses. (No need to chop the artichoke; the food processor will do it for you.) Season with hot sauce and salt and pepper to taste. Spoon into 5x5 or 6x6 baking dish sprayed with cooking spray. Bake for 30 to 40 minutes until golden brown and bubbly. Serve with chips, crackers, or veggie slices.

Belle Tip:

It's important to use the marinated artichokes for the fullest flavor!

174

And now these three remain: faith, hope and love.
But the greatest of these is love.

1 Corinthians 13:13 niv

◆–◆–◆–◆–◆–◆–◆–◆–◆–◆–◆–◆–◆–◆–◆–◆–◆–◆

*I*n the interest of healthy relationships, there are certain men who shouldn't be allowed to go shopping for their sweethearts without supervision. By certain men, I'm talking about Papa.

My parents recently celebrated their fiftieth wedding anniversary. Papa remembered this all on his own, which is good. He's been trying really hard ever since he got in trouble for bringing Mama flowers from the funeral home flower shop for their forty-ninth. That wasn't so good.

If you're thinking, *But, Shellie, people buy flowers from the funeral home for all kinds of happy occasions*, you have a point. The problem is someone at the establishment in question was either not paying attention, taking cruel advantage of Papa's shopping-challenged self, or having some fun at his expense. Regardless, they were wrong for letting the poor man purchase *a funeral spray* for his Sweet Thang! We're talking a nice-sized plastic spray meant to sit atop a casket or gravestone, the kind that comes with its own lovely base of green foam. Are you with me?

If you see Mama, don't tell her it's the thought that counts. We've tried that. She may have cut him some slack for those good intentions, too—if he weren't a repeat offender. Yes. It's hard to believe, but Papa made that same mistake for two years running, and for two years straight Mama toted the flowers to church and put them on the communion table, the one with the engraved "This Do in Remembrance of Me" line.

The rest of us are hoping that's just a funny little coincidence.

*S*peaking of payback, I once read a seriously funny. . .I mean sad. . .story from across the great pond. A man with very poor judgment made an appointment with a dentist—who also happened to be the woman he had just broken up with only days earlier. The fellow had a toothache. That would be past tense, as he no longer has a toothache. No, not one. Miss Dentist fixed that.

After placing her ex under heavy anesthesia, Miss Dentist locked the door and proceeded to pull all of his teeth. All. Of. Them. Unconfirmed reports have it that her office staff did wonder why they could hear their boss saying, "He loves me. . .he loves me not. . .he loves me. . .he loves me not." Okay, I made that last part up, but not the teeth-pulling tragedy. That's on police record.

I lost track of the story before Miss Dentist was sentenced, but last I heard she was facing prison time—and get this—she was not even bothering to deny her crime. Said Miss Dentist, "I tried to be professional and detach myself from my emotions, but when I saw him lying there, I just decided to take all of his teeth out." Whoopsy, daisy! My bad.

It's too late to warn that fellow, but I'm prepared to offer solid advice to any other male who might find himself with an ache in his tooth or—and I stress this point—any other part of his anatomy.

Four out of five of my female friends recommend not allowing your ex-girlfriend to put you under anesthesia for any reason at any time.

Super Sunday Chip and Dip

I've served this dip at Super Bowl parties and watched it disappear.
You can serve store-bought chips with it or make your own baked tortilla chips.
Just cut regular flour tortillas into 8 even wedges. Arrange them
on a cookie sheet and spray them with cooking oil. Sprinkle with salt
and bake at 400 degrees until lightly golden.

1 (15 ounce) can refried beans

1 tablespoon plus 1 teaspoon chili powder (or 1 package taco seasoning mix)

8 ounces cream cheese, softened

1 tablespoon lime juice

1 (4 ounce) can chopped green chilies

1 garlic clove, pressed

½ cup onion, finely chopped

1 (2.25 ounce) can chopped black olives

1¼ cups grated cheddar cheese

1 tablespoon fresh cilantro (or 1 teaspoon dried)

Preheat oven to 400 degrees. Combine refried beans and 1 teaspoon chili powder. Spread in bottom of small casserole dish. Combine cream cheese, lime juice, chilies, garlic, and remaining chili powder. Mix until smooth. Add onion, half of the black olives, and 1 cup cheddar cheese; mix well. Spread over beans. Bake 20 to 25 minutes or until hot. Top with remaining olives and cheese. Sprinkle with cilantro.

Smoking Fine Hot Wing Dip

Everybody I know loves buffalo chicken wings, mess and all. Here's a tailgating, crowd-pleasing option on that party favorite, only it comes in a dip! It's like eating buffalo chicken wings without the bones.

One pound of boneless chicken breasts

McCormick Chicken Rotisserie Seasoning

Pepper

Butter

1 tablespoon Worcestershire sauce

8 ounces cream cheese, cubed

½ cup bottled buffalo wing sauce

1 (4 ounce) container blue cheese crumbles

1 stalk celery, finely chopped

2 green onions, diced

1 jalapeño pepper, seeded and chopped

Rinse chicken breasts, dry, and rub thoroughly with McCormick Chicken Rotisserie Seasoning and black pepper. Place in cast-iron skillet, dot with butter, sprinkle with Worcestershire sauce, and bake at 350 degrees for 30 minutes. Cool. Pull meat into bite-size pieces and set aside. (Start with rotisserie chicken from your local grocery if you'd like.)

To prepare sauce, combine cubed cream cheese, buffalo wing sauce, blue cheese crumbles, celery, onion, and jalapeño pepper in glass mixing bowl. Microwave 2 minutes or until cheese begins to melt. Stir in chicken and bake at 350 degrees for 30 minutes so flavors can meld. Yum! Serve with your favorite crackers or chips!

Belle Tip:

You do know not to use dishwashing liquid to clean your cast-iron skillet, right? If you can't wipe it clean, try using a paste of salt and water, but don't let anyone come at your skillet with soap! It's a no-no!

Whatever your hand finds to do, do it with all your might.
ECCLESIASTES 9:10 NIV

You wouldn't have liked me when I was coaching girls' basketball. When I consider how I acted back then, I don't like that person much myself. Several years ago I wrote about that period of my life in one of my humor books. Here's that excerpt from *Sue Ellen's Girl Ain't Fat, She Just Weighs Heavy*:

> *Though I am now serving as the (reformed) Belle of All Things*
> *Southern, I was once a passionate girls' basketball coach and I*
> *may have been a teeny weensy bit hard on the referees. By teeny*
> *weensy I mean that I once tapped the official calling our contest on*
> *the shoulder and asked him what game he was watching because*
> *it certainly wasn't the one I was coaching. Yeah, he thought that*
> *deserved a technical, too. . . . The good news is that I got help. I went*
> *through a twelve-step program called "Zebras Are Our Friends."*

All joking aside, it took time and perspective to understand what I'm about to tell you, but over the years I've come to realize that my obsession with the referees impacted a lot of those ball games far more than any of the officiating I was anguishing over in the heat of the moment. Why do I say that? Because my preoccupation with the referees hindered my ability to help my players when they needed me the most. Sure, it's humbling to admit that, but I'm willing to do it in hopes that it will help us all see a larger, more important truth.

I think we can all have a tendency to act like that old basketball coaching me in regard to the situation of our world, our justice system, and yes, if we're honest—our politics. It can be tempting to obsess over fair and unfair, over left and right. As believers, however, we need to make sure we're not letting the latest debate take us out of the bigger picture, the game of life.

Let's not allow ourselves to be rendered ineffective in our greater call to help the hurting people around us. I'm not saying it's wrong for us to have an opinion. And I'm not saying we can't voice it. I just want us to remember that a dying world needs to hear less of our fiery rhetoric and more about the saving grace of our Savior.

Phil's Mushroom Chips with Homemade Jalapeño Ranch Dip

This dip and chip recipe carries my beloved hubby's name because it is one of his all-time favorite snacks. Don't make one without the other. The jalapeño ranch dip and those mushroom chips, Phil says, "need" each other.

DIP:

½ cup buttermilk

½ cup mayonnaise

2 jalapeño peppers, stemmed and seeded

2 teaspoons minced garlic

2 green onions, chopped

Juice of 1 lime

2 to 3 tablespoons chopped cilantro

Salt and pepper to taste

MUSHROOMS:

2 to 3 portobello mushrooms

½ to 1 cup flour

1 tablespoon Cajun seasoning

2 eggs, lightly beaten

1 cup panko bread crumbs

Nonstick cooking spray

Preheat oven to 425 degrees. Prepare dip by combining all ingredients in food processor. Once creamy liquid forms, chill.

Clean portobello mushrooms and slice into ¼-inch pieces. Prepare breading station with 3 bowls: one with flour seasoned with Cajun seasoning, one with 2 lightly beaten eggs, and one with panko bread crumbs.

To coat mushrooms, dredge in flour, dip in eggs, and dredge in bread crumbs. Arrange on baking sheet prepared with nonstick cooking spray. Bake 10 minutes or until slices are golden brown. Serve with homemade jalapeño ranch dip.

Nutty Pimiento Cheese Snacks

Cheese straws meet pimiento cheese in this wonderfully nutty recipe. The only problem I've found with them is making enough for the people who come back for seconds, and thirds, and. . .

24 slices party rye bread

½ cup grated sharp cheddar cheese

2 ounces cream cheese, softened

1 (2 ounce) jar diced pimientos, drained and chopped

Dash hot sauce

2 tablespoons finely chopped pecans

Place party rye bread slices on baking sheet and broil until lightly toasted. Cream together sharp cheddar and cream cheese. Stir in drained and chopped pimientos, hot sauce, and pecans.

Turn toasted bread slices and top with nutty cheese mixture. Broil until cheese is hot and bubbly. Enjoy!

Roasted Red Pepper Spread

I like to serve this simple spread on crackers or toasted french bread. You can use store-bought roasted peppers but, be warned, the flavor doesn't compare, and roasting peppers is super easy.

2 red bell peppers

8 ounces cream cheese, softened

3 tablespoons chopped fresh basil

2 cloves garlic, minced

2 tablespoons fresh lime juice

¼ teaspoon pepper

Dash sea salt

Wash peppers, remove seeds, slice in half, and place on foil-lined cookie sheet. Roast at 450 degrees for 20 to 25 minutes, let rest 30 minutes, remove skins, and chop.

Combine softened cream cheese with chopped basil, minced garlic, lime juice, pepper, salt, and chopped peppers. Blend in food processor until smooth. Chill for at least an hour to give flavors time to mingle.

Bodacious Bayou Olive Spread

Use this versatile olive spread as a topping for your favorite breads or on fresh green salads, sandwiches, and pastas. However you choose to serve it, once you do you'll reach for it again and again!

8 ounces cream cheese, softened

1 (4.25 ounce) can chopped black olives

1 teaspoon Worcestershire sauce

Dash Cajun seasoning

½ teaspoon lemon juice

½ cup finely chopped pecans (optional)

Dash hot sauce

Combine softened cream cheese with chopped black olives. Stir in Worcestershire sauce, Cajun seasoning, and lemon juice. Add chopped pecans and hot sauce. Spread on french bread and toast in 350-degree oven for 10 to 15 minutes.

MARINATED CHRISTMAS CHEESE BITES

My Marinated Christmas Cheese Bites will make a beautiful presentation at your holiday parties, dressed in their red and green colors, but they're not just for looks. These little babies are a cheese lover's delight.

½ cup olive oil

½ cup white wine vinegar

¼ cup fresh lime juice

1 small jar drained, roasted, and diced sweet red peppers

1 bunch green onions, diced

3 tablespoons chopped fresh cilantro

3 tablespoons chopped fresh parsley

1 teaspoon sugar

½ teaspoon each salt and pepper

1 (8 ounce) block sharp cheddar

1 (8 ounce) block Monterey Jack with peppers

1 (8 ounce) package cream cheese, chilled in freezer until firm

Prepare marinade by whisking together olive oil, white wine vinegar, and lime juice. Add sweet red peppers and green onions. Season with cilantro, parsley, sugar, salt, and pepper.

Chill cheeses for easier slicing. Cut each block in half lengthwise, then slice crosswise into ¼-inch slices. Cream cheese will slice best if chilled in freezer until firm.

Layer cheese, alternating varieties in a shallow casserole dish, and pour marinade across top. Cover tightly and chill at least 8 hours. Serve on a pretty dish with crackers. Spoon extra marinade over top.

Roasted Eggplant Zucchini Spread

This spread is the perfect answer when you need something quick and delicious. It packs in a ton of flavor and hits you with a delightful helping of vegetables and herbs!

1 large eggplant, sliced vertically, rinsed, and patted dry

1 large zucchini, sliced vertically, rinsed, and patted dry

1 cup and 1 tablespoon olive oil

1 teaspoon each salt and pepper

2 tablespoons white wine vinegar

1½ teaspoons minced roasted garlic

Pinch red pepper flakes

¼ teaspoon thyme

¼ teaspoon oregano

Juice of half a lemon

½ cup olive oil

Remove skin from eggplant and zucchini. Place both on roasting or baking pan, drizzle with about a tablespoon of olive oil, and season with salt and pepper. Roast at 400 degrees for 10 to 12 minutes. Remove and allow to cool.

Dice eggplant and zucchini and place in food processor. Add remaining ingredients except for olive oil. Pulse a few times until mixture is smooth. Then, slowly, with processor running, add 1 cup olive oil and process 1 minute or until desired consistency. Store in airtight container in refrigerator for up to a week (if it lasts that long!).

7

VEGGIES, SALADS, AND SIDES

DUCT TAPE AS A BEAUTY TOOL

When in doubt, overdress.
SOUTHERN MAMAS' SAYING

My most valued beauty and fitness tips come from my mother, beginning with her legendary advice, "Suck your stomach in and put some color on." I even used that stellar piece of wisdom as the title of my first humor book. It just felt right, seeing as how I'd heard it all of my life. I'm fond of saying that I slept with my stomach sucked in till I was nine months pregnant with my first child and I finally realized I was going to have to let things fall where they may, if you will. That said, I have never, and I mean never scoffed at mama's color line.

Lipstick is a big deal in our family.

It's why my ears perked up when I first heard about the "lipstick effect." In case you missed it, the lipstick effect theory says that lipstick sales go up during hard times and are therefore an indicator of how consumers are feeling about the economy. Experts claim women will forgo purchasing this season's must-have dress or boots, but they won't pass on their lip color,

and they'll even splurge on the more expensive lipstick brands. I don't know how much of that theory is valid here in the Deep South with women like myself who have been steeped in lipstick learning. Yours truly recently bought a costly lipstick system, and it had zero to do with the economy and everything to do with the fact that this stuff lives up to its claims—it lasts until you take it off. Period.

And yes, I did say lipstick *system*. We'll get back to that. As my readers and radio listeners have heard me whine about occasionally or five thousand times, my lips are sorta kinda on the thin side (meaning I can make a lizard look like she's had Botox).

But I mentioned the system. Well, that's the tricky part for a belle like me, and by that I mean someone with the attention span of a gnat on caffeine. You're supposed to apply three coats of the liquid color, allowing each coat a few seconds to dry before applying the next. Once this procedure is complete, you add your superglossy topcoat, unless you've made a boo-boo. If you've accidentally colored outside the lines, there's a third tube that will remove your mistake. Don't lose tube number three unless you want to walk around looking like you've had an extreme makeover from your four-year-old grandchild. What?

It's also important not to let your lips touch before they dry. No talking or your lips will be sealed, so to speak. I mentioned this to my man, and he said that would be a shame. He did not look sincere.

My friend Paulette is the one who told me about this system. She pointed out that gluing your lips together might be an easy way to drop a few pounds, so in her words, it's a win-win. I wonder what the experts would say to that.

The funny thing is that out of everything my Mama schooled my sisters and me on concerning feminine matters, she passed smooth over what we could expect at middle age and beyond. I wrote extensively about this in my second humor book, *Sue Ellen's Girl Ain't Fat, She Just Weighs Heavy*, and no, I'm not mentioning those titles on purpose to sell more books, but it does sound like a fine idea and bills do come around right regular.

Men-type readers, if you're with us, you may be tempted to skip the next few paragraphs once you recognize the subject matter. Don't do it. This could be educational to you in a "prepare yourself" sort of way. For my girlfriends out there, especially you middle-age marvels, brace yourselves. Someone has got to tell you these things, and our mamas are too busy ~~laughing at~~ loving us.

The latest medical findings suggest that many of us will experience hot flashes for up to fourteen years—twice as long as previously believed. Oh, joy. This is neither here nor there, but it'd help my feelings if we could all at least agree that this fiery phenomenon is woefully misnamed. "Hot flash" sounds warm and brief. They are neither. By the way, this isn't an invitation to flood my inbox or blow up my Facebook wall debating bioidentical versus synthetic hormone replacement. If you do that, I'll be tempted to pull your fingers off.

As you can see, I'm happy to report that this stage of life is not affecting my disposition. I'm still my same sweet self. But the subject of dismembering people does seem to keep cropping up around me. Recently I was giving a speech to several thousand women. They were a great crowd, totally engaged in my stories, which was only serving to egg me on. I couldn't tell 'em fast enough.

To stage right of me stood a woman tasked with translating my message into sign language. If you've ever heard me speak, you know that I can get, well, into it. I was told afterward that watching that dear lady keep up with me was entertaining in and of itself. So much so, that many in the audience who didn't need her services found themselves watching her, too.

At one point during my remarks, I mentioned that airline prank I played on my best buddy that made her want to pull my arm off and whoop me with it (see pages 74–75). After a brief pause, the translator took her left hand and performed a sawing motion at her right shoulder. Then she took that imaginary severed arm and began beating herself around the head with it. They don't call those folks sign-language experts for nothing.

SALT AND PEPPER PARMESAN SNAP PEAS FROM KITCHEN BELLEICIOUS

Snap peas are nothing new to the South, but this recipe is extra special. It may not be the fanciest or cleverest dish, but it is an easy dish with simple ingredients you should already have on hand. The recipe packs a boatload of flavor, and I call that a winner! Try this super-simple vegetable dish and you won't be disappointed.

6 tablespoons butter, softened

2 teaspoons sea salt

2 teaspoons freshly cracked black pepper

½ cup grated parmesan cheese

1 cup pecan pieces

1½ pounds sugar snap peas, washed

Mix together butter, salt, pepper, and parmesan cheese. Toss pecans with half this mixture. Roast pecans at 350 degrees for 10 minutes. Set aside. Coat peas with remaining butter mixture. Bake at 400 degrees for 12 to 14 minutes. Remove from oven and toss with pecans. Serve warm.

Simply Delicious Candied Carrots

I've never really been a fan of candied carrots—at least until I started cooking them with balsamic vinegar and tossing 'em with feta cheese. Things changed quickly after that. These little darlings earned themselves a place at my table.

1½ pounds carrots

3 tablespoons balsamic vinegar

3 tablespoons olive oil

2 tablespoons brown sugar

Salt and pepper

4 ounces feta cheese, crumbled

Lemon juice

Cut carrots lengthwise into long, thin strips. Whisk together balsamic vinegar and olive oil. Add brown sugar. Toss carrots in dressing, place on lightly greased cookie sheet, and sprinkle with salt and pepper.

Bake at 400 degrees for 40 to 45 minutes or until vegetables are tender and browned, stirring every 15 minutes. Transfer to serving platter and gently toss with lemon juice and feta.

Belle Tip:

If your family aren't feta fans, you can skip the cheese and still have tasty carrots!

You can't lose weight by talking about it. You have to keep your mouth shut.
— OLD FARMER'S ALMANAC

CAJUN GREEN BEANS WITH PEPPERED BACON

You're going to want to bookmark this page or carve this recipe into the dining room table, whatever it takes to keep it on hand. My family thinks it rocks your average green beans!

5 to 6 slices thick-cut pepper bacon

½ cup diced white onion

2 pounds green beans, trimmed (or one 32-ounce bag frozen green beans)

1 small carton mushrooms

Salt and pepper to taste

1½ tablespoons Tony Chachere's Original Creole Seasoning

2 tablespoons white grape juice plus dash of lemon juice (or white cooking wine)

Cook bacon in cast-iron skillet. Remove, drain, and break into bite-size pieces, reserving grease in skillet. Add diced onion to bacon grease and sauté until soft. Add frozen green beans and mushrooms. (Fresh beans are wonderful if they are available, but if not, skip the cans and use frozen—more nutrients.) Season beans with salt and pepper and Tony Chachere's Original Creole Seasoning. Add white grape juice and a dash of lemon juice (or use white wine in place of juices). Cover and cook until beans soften. Transfer to serving dish, top with chopped bacon, and toss lightly.

Bacon is duct tape for the kitchen.
UNKNOWN

Southerners love a good tale. They are born reciters, great memory retainers, diary keepers, letter exchangers, letter savers, history tracers and debaters and— outstaying all the rest—great talkers.

EUDORA WELTY

●━━━━━━━━━━━━━━━━━━━━━━━━━━━●

I allowed a respectable amount of time to pass before I ever broached the next subject on my radio show, as the practice in question has led to at least one reported fatality. Besides, I really thought the straight running crazy trend would have played out by now, but no. You can find news reports on it all the time, so let's chat, shall we?

I can't get over the fact that people are doing things like injecting chicken fat into their backsides to give themselves bigger derrieres. Yes, ma'am, on purpose.

I've researched this thoroughly, meaning I googled and quizzed my beautician 'cause I knew she'd have the lowdown on it (and she did). As far as we can figure, it's still quite rare here in the South. Thankfully, we're still eating the chicken in these parts, but we can't let this sort of madness go unchecked. It could infect us all.

I mean, who came up with this? Was she standing in the kitchen injecting her butterball and watching that big thigh swell up when she thought, *Hmm. . .why not?* Personally, I can think of a hundred dozen reasons why not, as can every female in my circle of friends and family. We've dedicated our lives to reducing that area. Paulette is even willing to offer her fat as a better option, long as she doesn't have to pay for its removal. She claims hers has got to be a better grade than chicken fat as it is so tenacious. I know—we roll our eyes at her, too.

But hey, should you have your heart set on a larger derriere, I'm here to help, too, and my way is considerably less painful. I've designed a special diet to help you reach your goal, and I'm willing to share it for the amazingly low cost of $19.99. It's built around homemade ice cream, brownies, and Mama's Naner Pudding; and it's guaranteed to increase your rear end. Course, it'll also pad my bottom line, but that's just gravy, so to speak.

$\mathcal{S}$peaking of the lengths we humans will go to for approval, can we talk about the pouty lips and smiling selfies streaming endlessly on our social media walls? I'll be gentle. Some of my most favorite people in all the world post selfies regularly, so this is me proceeding respectfully and very carefully.

Are we good? Okay, consider this. Somewhere around 93 million selfies are posted daily. The numbers differ according to who's counting and what platforms are being included, and—Lord have mercy on my soul—that's not even counting the belfies (if you don't know what a belfie is, count your blessings and ignore that reference). Still, by anyone's accounting, we're posting a whole lot of duck lips. It all begs the question:

What in the world?

The group shot snagged selfie-style because everyone wants to be in the picture is one thing, as is the special event selfie, and maybe even the occasional selfie itself. But what is fueling the need to consistently and repetitively pose alone and share our images with the world?

What are we to make of this?

If a picture is worth a thousand words, could it be we're looking at humankind's incessant need to be seen, noticed, and/or acknowledged? I think so. And yet the fullest, grandest life is found not in being acknowledged but in acknowledging and beholding Jesus the Mediator, the meeting place between God and humans.

As followers of this Jesus, we've been called to die to self, not to promote it, but my experience has been that self has a thousand lives. Amen?

I don't claim to have all the answers, but I do have an idea. The next time we're tempted to broadcast our own face, let's stop and seek His. If ever something needed to go viral, we're looking at it. #SeekHisFace could change the world.

Shellie's Homestyle Scalloped Potatoes

This is the type of dish I stir up during our busiest farming seasons. When my hardworking man is planting or harvesting, when the hours are long and the days are running into each other, it's time for one of his favorite comfort foods—scalloped potatoes.

2 pounds potatoes
1 medium yellow onion
Salt and pepper to taste
½ to 1 stick butter
1 cup grated cheddar cheese
¾ to 1 cup heavy cream
Green onions

Wash and thinly slice potatoes, leaving skins on. Peel and slice onion as thinly as possible. Layer half of potatoes and onions in casserole dish. Sprinkle with salt and pepper. Scatter a few pats of butter over top along with half of grated cheddar. Repeat layers. Pour heavy whipping cream over top layer. (This isn't exactly a diet dish. Just keep reminding yourself that moderation is the key!) Cover with foil and bake at 350 degrees for 50 to 60 minutes or until potatoes are fork tender. Remove foil and let top brown. Sprinkle with chopped green onions and serve hot.

The sleep of a laborer is sweet.
ECCLESIASTES 5:12 NIV

$\mathcal{I}$ was dragging my tired self back to another hotel room when I got a text message from my son-in-law with a perspective from my then-four-year-old grandson, Grant Thomas, that brought with it a much-appreciated belly laugh.

Patrick's text read: SO, WE'RE WATCHING THE TEXANS. THEY BREAK TO COMMERCIAL AND THEY'RE PANNING THE CHEERLEADERS WHEN GRANT SEES A BROWN-HAIRED CHEERLEADER AND SHOUTS, "HEY, THERE'S KEGGIE!" (My grandmother name.)

As I mentioned when I tweeted that story out to the universe—oh, please, you know I couldn't miss that opportunity—this very weary Keggie wasn't feeling anything like a Texas cheerleader that night, but I simply adored the ATS Beau Czar for thinking I could hang. (I made all of my grandchildren czars because I could.)

Only a darling grandson could make that kind of mistake. It's not that I'm obese, but I've had to be extra diligent about fighting the middle-age spread ever since I had that little body-image epiphany. I was trying to self-talk myself out of a fat mood. "You're fine," I said to myself. "You're in the same size pants you've always worn."

I felt pretty good about that, too, until myself replied, "Look in the mirror, Miss Muffin. You may be *in* the same pants, but you're over and around them, too." *Whatever.*

The point is, that even if I wanted to get in one of those itty-bitty uniforms, and I don't, I wouldn't stand a chance of pulling it off without some serious liposuction and/or duct tape. It does, however, remind me of another good story.

As you may have picked up on, I'm all about trying to stay in shape. Mama taught us girls that it was wrong for us to let ourselves blow up (that's a southern term meaning to let oneself go), and I do everything I can to live by that admonition. That said, I contend that our society, as a whole, has taken the idea of a healthy body image too far.

I ripped this next bit straight from the headlines, "Mommies are hiring personal trainers for their offspring." I know. The article was even more alarming. It went on to say that children as young as five are now working with personal trainers.

Friends, we're not talking about city people who don't have a backyard for their kiddos to play in, or I wouldn't dream of, well, weighing in. I realize city people can't lock their young'uns outside like I did and my mama did before me.

I still remember my own kids' wee faces as they tried to slide the patio door open from the outside, with their little lips mouthing the words, "It's locked."

"I know," I would tell them. "Now, shoo!"

But let's get real. Hiring Suzie Q a personal trainer at $85 an hour? That points to other problems. Here's a clue: one of the parents being interviewed said, "My child is benefiting from the one-on-one activity." You think?

Before this trend goes any further and someone starts thinking about circuit training those adorable potbellies off my grandbabies and I have a fit and fall out, perhaps we could all take a cue from some folks at the other end of the aging spectrum.

I saw a piece on the news not long ago about a group of nursing home residents who gave the staff the slip and snuck out to a biker's bar! They needed some R & R, and someone in the group apparently thought leather, pink hair, and fake tattoos would be just what the doctor ordered.

While there's a lot about biker seniors that makes me smile, I'm not advocating hitting the bar scene. I'm just saying that many of the obesity trends in this country could be reversed if we all followed the biker grannies' lead and just got up and started moving. Or, as one mature biker babe put it when reporting on the activities of her ninety-seven-year-old friend who took to the dance floor with her walker, "She shook her booty, and she shook it good!"

Have Mercy Butternut Squash

If you've been passing right on by that big gorgeous butternut squash in the supermarket, it's time to hit the brakes. Butternut squash just needs the tiniest bit of tender loving care to deliver big-time taste. One taste and you'll understand why I call this recipe my Have Mercy Butternut Squash.

1 butternut squash

2 to 3 tablespoons olive oil

1 teaspoon sea salt

1 teaspoon pepper

2 to 3 teaspoons minced garlic

1 to 2 tablespoons finely chopped cilantro

1 to 2 tablespoons fresh lime juice

Wash and peel squash. Slice in half lengthwise, remove seeds, and cut into 1/2- to 1-inch cubes. Spread squash in single layer on baking sheet, drizzle with olive oil, and season with sea salt and pepper. Now is not the time to get all miserly with that salt and pepper. I use a good bit, say at least a teaspoon each. . .or more. Spoon minced garlic over top and toss until all cubes are coated with olive oil. Bake at 400 degrees for 1 hour. To serve, transfer to bowl and toss with cilantro and lime juice. *Have mercy!*

Belle Tip:

If some of the cubes get a little charred, don't even worry. My man and I love that extra crunch!

Have you heard of the garlic diet? You don't lose much weight, but from a distance your friends think you look thinner.

Unknown

BAKED EGGPLANT WITH GARLIC CHEESE TOPPING

I'll be honest with you. I wasn't all that fond of eggplant until I found this recipe. I'm pretty sure it was the garlic cheese that ended up sealing the deal!

1 large eggplant

2 teaspoons extra virgin olive oil

1 tablespoon pesto

½ tablespoon balsamic vinegar

1 cup cherry tomatoes

4 ounces garlic cheese

Fresh basil

Salt to taste

Freshly ground black pepper to taste

Trim stem off and halve eggplant lengthwise. With sharp knife, make slices in pulp for moisture to escape—like you might do with a piecrust. Sprinkle both halves with salt and let rest a half hour or so. Water will form on top. Blot with paper towel. Place eggplant halves on baking sheet and brush well with olive oil. Bake at 400 degrees for 30 to 40 minutes or until tender.

Combine pesto with balsamic vinegar. Once eggplant is tender, cover with diced cherry tomatoes and drizzle with pesto and vinegar sauce. Sprinkle with garlic cheese, chopped basil, and salt and pepper to taste. Bake another 8 to 10 minutes or until cheese is thoroughly melted.

Mrs. Joyce's Squash Dressing

Mrs. Joyce is Mama's good friend and neighbor. She brought this dish over during Mama's back surgery. Until then I didn't even think I liked squash dressing. Mrs. Joyce made a believer out of me. And, it gets better— she shared the recipe. So now I get to make a believer out of y'all!

1 package Martha Washington corn bread mix

1 pound hot sausage

6 to 8 yellow summer squash, washed and sliced into bite-size pieces

1 bell pepper, washed and sliced into bite-size pieces

1 onion, diced

¼ cup butter

½ pound Velveeta

1 can cream of chicken soup

1 (4 ounce) jar pimientos

Prepare homemade corn bread or a skillet of Martha Washington corn bread mix. Brown sausage and drain grease. Steam squash, bell pepper, and onion in butter until tender. Stir in Velveeta cheese. When cheese melts, add cream of chicken soup and pimientos.

Add cooked and crumbled corn bread and drained sausage. Stir together well and bake at 350 degrees for 30 minutes or until heated through and top is golden brown. Mrs. Joyce says this recipe usually feeds twelve—unless they're big strapping men. I say a few women could make a serious dent in it, too.

There's no accounting for some of the health and beauty trends making the news these days. My last "You've got to be kidding me moment" began innocently enough as I was researching one of the latest trends that has women—young women—dying their hair gray on purpose. I understand women who decide not to fight the upkeep thing and just go gray naturally. Although, as I've said in the past, they'll have to pry Miss Clairol light neutral brown from my cold dead hands before I give in, but I admit to being completely bumfuzzled as to why young girls would ever be interested in accelerating the process.

And yet, dear ones, I have now realized that the choice to go gray at any early age isn't really all that bizarre, at least not when we're talking about our crowning glory. There are crazier things afoot. Lean in.

I have recently learned that there are women the world over letting their armpit hair grow out so they can dye it in various attention-getting shades, such as pink, purple, and green. I do not recommend googling this for verification. Trust me. You can't unsee this stuff.

Once I recovered from my initial shock, I called the Golden Girls to get their reaction. Again, that would be Mama and her sisters. (I'd love to quote Aunt Marleta's response in particular, but Mama would have my hide.) Let's just say the Golden Girls won't be jumping on this particular bandwagon.

I also conducted an informal Facebook poll to see just how far-reaching this armpit movement is among the women in the All Things Southern community. I'm pleased to report that it has not caught on with our fellow belles. With the exception of that one sweet thang who noted the cost of upkeep and how difficult it would be to color-coordinate the look with her summer wardrobe—and I do believe she was just funnin'—to a southern soul, none of the girls were interested.

Not even when I told them that the feminists report that letting your armpit hair grow out is powerful! As Paulette noted, "It'll be powerful all right. Powerfully stanky."

The girl is spot on this time. It be hot down here in the summertime.

We tend to talk slow in the South
because it's too hot to talk faster.
UNKNOWN

*M*ost of us have given in to the doctors' warnings about trying to achieve that golden glow. There are some holdouts. . . .

My cousin Michelle is, by her own account, a professional tanner. Not long ago Michelle asked me for a strange favor. Should she not be tanned when she passed, Michelle wanted to know if I would mind taking her in for a spray job before the funeral. Yes, she sure did mean after the fact, and yes, I did mind. Let the record show that I made no such promise.

One of Michelle's legendary tanning stories occurred when she and one of her husbands were living in Texas. (Michelle has kind of collected husbands over the years, but it's legal. She always gets rid of one before marrying another.) Cousin Michelle left that particular city and that particular husband after the following incident, albeit for different reasons.

The day of the big tanning debacle, my stressed-out cousin had decided that a tanning-bed session was exactly what the doctor ordered to make her feel better. So, during her lunch break, Michelle headed to the city's newest tanning salon. Upon her arrival, a receptionist attempted to launch into her new-customer instructions, but Michelle waved the young, flat-bellied girl off—what with her being a professional tanner and all. "Just point me to my room," our expert instructed.

Soon Michelle was disrobing in a large room while admiring the big picture window facing one of the city's busy downtown streets. *Cool! One-way glass*, Michelle thought to herself. *These people have thought of everything.*

Michelle was systematically applying lotion to every inch of her toned, tanned physique when a young boy rode by on his bike and promptly crashed into the brick wall. *Ouch! He should watch where he's going*, Michelle noted. She turned away from the window and continued her professional lotion routine. Once, she glanced over her shoulder to discover that traffic had become quite congested, but even then Michelle decided that something interesting was probably painted on the side of the building. She made a mental note to check it out when she left.

Prep finally completed, Michelle was climbing her nude body into the sunbed when she noticed the small sign above the light switch that read TO LOWER SCREEN MOUNTED BEHIND WINDOW VALANCE, PRESS HERE.

No doubt, that tidbit was in those earlier instructions our family tanning expert had chosen to disregard.

Michelle said I could share this story if I apologized to the state of Texas for her and included a warning: "Strip tanning is for professionals. Please don't try this at home."

While I personally gave up tanning beds years ago, that doesn't mean I've totally accepted the Snow White look. A couple of summers ago I was getting ready to do some book events when one of my author friends recommended I get a spray tan. She loves hers, says she just rotates in front of these little spigots and gets an even, natural-looking glow. What could go wrong, right? I decided to give it an early try in preparation for an important speaking engagement.

I googled spray tans, chose the one that sounded the least like a high school hangout, and plugged the address into my Garmin. Shortly thereafter I was standing at a counter speaking to a sweet young girl who called herself the operator. As Papa might say, "She was still wet behind the ears."

My heart sank to discover I had misread their advertisement. They didn't have the automatic spray machine, after all. Miss Thang told me I'd have to get nekked and she would personally spray me. I assume my apprehension registered on my face, because she quickly added that she didn't mind. That's a direct quote, y'all. She said, "I don't mind."

So, I thought to myself, *this is what it has come to—Miss Thang would not mind seeing me in my birthday suit.* It was a no thanks for me, and as I said to my best friend, I didn't know whether to laugh or cry.

For the record, my loyal BFF was not so torn. She giggled for days.

I minded that, big-time.

Friends are the bacon bits in the salad bowl of life.
Unknown

Shellie's Chicken Salad Potpie

I'm not a big potpie girl. On the other hand, I do like the concept of a potpie and I am a huge chicken salad fan, so one evening I thought, Why not a chicken salad potpie? *I have to say it was one of my more brilliant inspirations.*

1 (9 inch) pie shell

1½ cups mayonnaise

1 teaspoon pepper

¼ teaspoon salt

1 tablespoon lemon juice

½ cup grated sharp cheddar cheese

½ cup chopped pecans

1½ cups celery, finely chopped

1 bunch green onions, diced

2 cups diced cooked chicken

1 cup crushed potato chips for topping

Bake refrigerated piecrust per package instructions, or make your own crust. While piecrust cools, in mixing bowl combine mayonnaise, pepper, salt, and lemon juice. Stir in cheddar, chopped pecans, celery, and green onions.

Add diced chicken. (Bake your own chicken or use rotisserie chicken from the store.) Combine all ingredients in prebaked pie shell and top with crushed potato chips. Bake at 350 degrees for 25 minutes. Yum! Indeed!

CRUNCHY ROMAINE SALAD

Salads do not have to be boring! My Crunchy Romaine Salad benefits from nuts, ramen noodles, and bacon! It puts the basic lettuce and tomato salad to shame.

SALAD:

3 tablespoons butter

1 package ramen noodles

3 to 6 slices bacon, cooked and crumbled

1 cup pecans or almonds, chopped

1 head Romaine lettuce, cleaned and torn into bite-size pieces

1 head broccoli, coarsely chopped

1 bunch green onions, chopped

SWEET AND SOUR DRESSING:

1 cup vegetable oil

¼ cup sugar

½ cup red wine vinegar

3 teaspoons soy sauce

Salt and pepper to taste

Melt butter in cast-iron skillet. Break up ramen noodles and cook in melted butter for 2 to 3 minutes before adding crumbled bacon and pecans. Once nuts are brown, set crunchy mix aside.

For salad base, tear Romaine into bite-size pieces. Add broccoli and green onions. Stir in noodles and almonds.

Prepare dressing by whisking together vegetable oil, sugar, red wine vinegar, and soy sauce. Add salt and pepper to taste. Dress your salad and enjoy!

BELLE TIP:

If you have peppered bacon on hand, all the better!

Jewish mothers dispense chicken soup; southern belles dispense chicken salad.

MARILYN SCHWARTZ

Cajun Tater Salad

My family raves over my Cajun Tater Salad. It's got flavor galore, and it's so hearty that it's practically a meal in itself.

SALAD:

2 pounds small red potatoes
½ cup chopped red onion
¾ cup chopped green onions
¼ cup chopped fresh parsley
3 tablespoons cider vinegar
½ pound Cajun sausage
1 tablespoon olive oil

DRESSING:

3 tablespoons cider vinegar
3 tablespoons olive oil
1 tablespoon Dijon mustard
2 cloves garlic, crushed
Salt and pepper
½ teaspoon cayenne pepper

Boil new potatoes in salted water until tender (about 25 minutes). Rinse in cold water and set aside to cool completely.

When cool, slice potatoes into chips and toss lightly with red onion, green onion, parsley, and cider vinegar. Sauté sausage in cast-iron skillet with tablespoon of olive oil. When sausage is fully cooked and browned, remove with slotted spoon, saving drippings.

Prepare dressing by whisking cider vinegar into sausage drippings along with 3 tablespoons olive oil, Dijon mustard, garlic, salt, pepper, and cayenne pepper. Stir dressing until it boils, and toss with potatoes and sausage mixture.

Belle Tip:

Letting your potatoes cool is very important. If you don't, they'll be mushy and ugly. (That's probably where we get the phrase "Cool your taters"! Wait, that's "Cool your jets." Never mind.)

Marinated Broccoli Salad

I love me some broccoli. I'll eat it a number of ways. My hubby—not so much.
But he'll eat my Marinated Broccoli Salad any day of the week.

4 cloves garlic

1 teaspoon salt

½ cup olive oil

¼ cup red wine vinegar

1 tablespoon Dijon mustard

1 bunch broccoli, cut into florets

1 head red leaf lettuce

1 (4.5 ounce) package bacon pieces

½ cup bread crumbs

½ cup grated parmesan cheese

Peel 4 garlic cloves. Place in small bowl, sprinkle with salt, then mash garlic and salt until paste forms. Add garlic paste to olive oil, red wine vinegar, and Dijon mustard. Stir well, pour over broccoli florets, and toss to coat. Chill for at least 3 hours to allow flavors to meld.

To prepare salad, add marinated florets and bacon pieces to lettuce. Sprinkle with bread crumbs, top with grated parmesan cheese, and enjoy!

The man who invented instant grits also thought of frozen fried chicken, and they ought to lock him up before he tries to freeze-dry collards.

Lewis Grizzard

Baby Butter Potatoes with Herbs

Here's a great side dish that meets all my requirements. It will reward you with tons of flavor without requiring a huge investment of your time. For the record, I am nuts over these little bite-size spuds, y'all. It's really easy to infuse them with flavor.

1½ pounds baby dutch potatoes

2 tablespoons butter

2 tablespoons olive oil

Salt and pepper

1 teaspoon minced garlic

2 tablespoons each fresh rosemary, chives, and parsley

Clean and scrub baby dutch potatoes. Add to pot of boiling water. When water returns to boil, turn down and let potatoes simmer. When fork tender, drain and pat potatoes dry so butter, olive oil, and herbs stick to skins.

Combine butter and olive oil in cast-iron skillet. Add potatoes and season with salt, pepper, and garlic, tossing lightly to brown on all sides. Once skins are crispy and brown, remove with slotted spoon while still hot, put in serving dish, and toss with rosemary, chives, and parsley.

Cajun Grits

The way I see it, any recipe that begins with grits has a head start. In this dish, grits team up with bacon and tomatoes to go beyond the breakfast table and serve as a side dish for your noon or evening meal.

½ pound bacon

1 bell pepper, chopped

1 onion, chopped

1 (10 ounce) can Ro-Tel tomatoes

1½ cups quick cooking grits (not instant)

Fry bacon; drain, crumble, and hide it. (Every cotton-pickin' time I cook with bacon, my hungry bunch comes through, and it disappears before I can get it in the dish.) Reserve bacon grease.

Sauté chopped green peppers and onions in reserved drippings. When vegetables are tender, add can of Ro-Tel tomatoes and simmer a few minutes to draw out flavor. Cook grits according to package directions and add to tomatoes, onions, and peppers. Top with crumbled bacon and serve.

Okra. Corn. and Tomatoes

Few recipes are more quintessentially southern than Okra, Corn, and Tomatoes. You can make it with canned or frozen veggies, but it reaches its flavor peak when you can take advantage of summertime's abundant fresh produce.

2 cups fresh corn

3 to 5 ripe tomatoes

1 small onion, grated

1 tablespoon brown sugar, firmly packed

½ pound fresh okra, trimmed and cut into ½-inch slices

In heavy saucepan, combine all ingredients and simmer covered until okra is tender.

Gardening is cheaper than therapy and you get tomatoes.

UNKNOWN

Solid Gold Corn Dish

The name of this dish reminds me of a show my sisters and I watched on Saturday mornings back in the day—Soul Train. Or, as they said it, "Soulllllllllll Trainnnnnnnnnnnnnnnnn!" It's where we girls got our moves, that is, until Papa came in and decided he didn't much care for the moves we were getting. No more Soul Train, at least not when Papa was in the vicinity.

1 pound hot bulk pork sausage

1 bag frozen diced onions and peppers

3 tablespoons butter

3 tablespoons flour

1 cup milk

2 (11 ounce) cans Mexi-corn, drained

1 (10 ounce) can Ro-Tel tomatoes

2 cups cooked rice

1 pound Mexican Velveeta

1 teaspoon garlic powder

Cajun seasoning

Salt and pepper

Brown sausage with frozen veggie blend. Drain and set aside. Melt butter in cast-iron skillet. Whisk in flour, stir till well blended, add milk. Cook over medium heat until it begins to thicken. Return sausage to skillet and add Mexi-corn, tomatoes, cooked rice, and cubed Velveeta. Cook until Velveeta melts, stirring constantly.

Season with garlic powder, Cajun seasoning, and salt and pepper. Pour into casserole dish for baking. Your family is gonna love the combination of rice and cheese with that sausage and corn. Bake at 350 degrees for 20 to 30 minutes. Enjoy!

Homestyle Stovetop Mac and Cheese from Kitchen Belleicious

Macaroni and cheese is an iconic family dish that leaves you feeling good. Because this recipe is so simple to make, I like to splurge on it and use only the best cheeses—and lots of 'em. My homestyle mac and cheese is loaded with flavor, thanks to four cheeses along with coarse ground mustard and cracked black pepper.

- 32 ounces of your favorite small pasta (I use shells)
- 5 tablespoons unsalted butter
- ¼ cup flour
- 2 cups whole milk, warm to the touch
- 3 teaspoons coarse ground mustard or spicy Dijon mustard
- ¼ cup white wine (or white cooking wine or chicken broth)
- 1 teaspoon Worcestershire sauce
- ½ teaspoon paprika
- ½ teaspoon garlic powder
- ½ teaspoon salt
- ¾ teaspoon cracked black pepper
- 4 ounces sharp cheddar cheese, grated
- 4 ounces pepper jack cheese, grated
- 3 ounces white cheddar cheese, grated
- 4 ounces muenster cheese, grated

Prepare pasta according to package directions.

In large sauté pan or skillet, melt butter over medium heat. Add flour and stir constantly for about 3 minutes, until smooth. Pour in 1 cup milk in thin stream while whisking. It might start out lumpy, but keep whisking and it will smooth out into a thick paste. Add remaining milk and whisk until smooth. Add mustard and white wine and stir until combined. Stir in remaining seasonings and then cheeses (a little at a time) until all cheese is melted. Adjust taste if necessary with more or less salt.

Add drained pasta and gently mix. Enjoy mac and cheese hot off the stove or pour into a 9x13 pan sprayed with cooking spray and bake at 350 degrees for 20 minutes. Don't forget to top it with more cheese if you bake it!

Southern-Style Bourbon Baked Beans from Kitchen Belleicious

Whether you are southern or not, these beans will speak to your heart, satisfy your stomach, and automatically propel you to authentic southern cook status. Yes, I realize I'm really caking it on, but this is serious stuff. Caramelized onions, crispy but still chewy bacon, and a hint of tanginess and richness from the bourbon turn casual beans into something magical. I don't know a man who doesn't like baked beans, and as my grandmother/ mom/aunt/any southern woman will tell you, the way to a man's heart is through his stomach. Stir these up, and you'll be dearly loved!

8 slices bacon, roughly chopped

½ onion, chopped

2 tablespoons Dijon mustard

1 tablespoon Worcestershire sauce

3 tablespoons molasses

⅓ cup brown sugar

½ cup ketchup

¼ cup barbecue sauce

1 tablespoon apple cider vinegar

2 tablespoons good bourbon

1 teaspoon each salt and pepper

1 teaspoon Cajun seasoning

1 (28 ounce) can baked beans

In a medium skillet, cook bacon and onion until bacon is slightly crisp and onion is tender. Remove from heat. Place beans in large stockpot or oven-safe baking dish. Combine remaining ingredients with bacon and onion mixture. Stir into beans. Pour into deep dish you plan to serve from or leave in stockpot. Sprinkle with brown sugar.

Place in 350-degree oven and bake 45 minutes. Increase temperature to 425 degrees for 10 minutes to crisp bacon. Remove from oven and allow to rest about 5 minutes before serving.

MawMaw Lucy's
Crock-Pot Cheese Soufflé

*This last recipe is a tribute to the memory of a great southern cook and
my late mother-in-law, Lucy Lowry Tomlinson. She was quite a character!
I remember being a young bride and thinking that Lucy's Crock-Pot Cheese
Soufflé sounded a little too tricky for my skills. Little did I know it was a
layer and pour type of thing. You'll love the flavor of this dish, and you'll
enjoy serving something that might not be in your normal rotation of recipes.*

14 slices fresh bread

3 cups grated sharp cheese
(not preshredded)

2 tablespoons butter

6 eggs

3 cups milk (or half-and-half)

2 tablespoons Worcestershire
sauce

Salt and pepper to taste

½ teaspoon paprika

Grease slow cooker with butter. Remove crusts from
bread and tear bread into bite-size pieces. Place half of
bread in slow cooker and top with half of grated cheese
and 1 tablespoon butter. Note: don't use preshredded
cheese in this dish. It won't give you the same flavor or
consistency.

Repeat steps using remaining bread, cheese, and
butter. Beat eggs and blend with milk or half-and-half.
(Half-and-half will give a creamier consistency.)

Add Worcestershire sauce to eggs and milk along
with salt and pepper. Pour over bread and cheese and
sprinkle top with paprika. Cover and cook on low for 4
to 5 hours.

Belle Tip:

You can save those ends to make homemade
croutons. Try adapting my Corn Bread
Croutons recipe on page 84.

So Long, Don't Be a Stranger

I've so enjoyed sharing my recipes with you in these pages, along with stories of my family and friends. I hope you'll get in touch and stay in touch, because you feel like family. And on that note, I'd like to tell you one last story and speak a blessing over you before I go.

"Open wide! Here comes the airplane!"

Remember that line? It's from a mealtime game most of us have played with a wee one at one point or another. The spoon is the circling airplane, and the child's mouth is the hangar. The object? To get the hesitant youngster in question to allow another bite of whatever food you're offering into his or her mouth.

Should you find yourself feeding my youngest grandchild, Weston the Wonder Boy, you will quickly realize that playing this particular game is unnecessary. Weston is very willing to open his mouth wide. Your challenge will lie more along the line of shoveling the food in fast enough to please him. As of this writing, Wonder Boy is two years old, but the boy child has been eating like a farmhand from the first day he was offered solid food. None of us has ever really seen Weston get full. He simply gets removed from the table when his little belly starts looking like it may explode. That would also be when he is taken away from the dining area completely. (Total removal is necessary, because as long as Wonder Boy can still see food, he thinks he should be eating it.)

In Psalm 81:10 (NIV) God said to the children of Israel, "Open wide your mouth and I will fill it." I love that divine offer. It stands for all of God's people for all of time, you and me included. And from the context of the passage, we can see that God is talking about much more than physical food. He is encouraging the people to look to Him for fulfillment, provision, and direction. The promise is that if they will seek Him first, He will satisfy their longings.

Sadly, over the next few verses, we can also see that the children of Israel declined God's gracious offer. They turned a deaf ear to their Deliverer and, in turn, God backed away and allowed them to take their fill of the rotting culture around them. The question for you and me is, what will we do with God's invitation? If this world is what we crave, I'm afraid God will allow us to fill up on it. Let's not do it. Let's not be found making the same tragic mistake the children of Israel made all those years ago.

Okay, that's the story. Here's the blessing: *May you and I have a God-appetite modeled after Weston the Wonder Boy. May we live eager Jesus-hungry lives, opening our mouths wide and asking God to feed us with the Bread of Life.*

Hugs,
Shellie

How sweet are Your words to my taste!
Yes, sweeter than honey to my mouth!
PSALM 119:103 NASB

Recipe Index

SWEETS

SOUPS, SAUCES, AND TOPPINGS

ABOUT THE AUTHOR

An incurable storyteller, down-home southern cook, and bona fide people lover, Shellie Rushing Tomlinson enjoys entertaining and encouraging a wide range of audiences. Whether sharing her recipes and her humorous slant on growing up southern on the radio and via her popular website http://www .allthingssouthern.com, speaking in civic and educational settings, or offering inspiring thoughts in church retreats and ladies' seminars, Shellie's talks are always full of laughs, inspiration, and motivation.

Shellie Rushing Tomlinson lives in Lake Providence, Louisiana, with her husband, Phil. They have two children and five grandchildren. Shellie is the author of three self-published titles, *Lessons Learned on Bull Run Road*, *'Twas the Night before the Very First Christmas*, *Southern Comfort with Shellie Rushing Tomlinson,* and two nonfiction books with Penguin Group USA, *Suck Your Stomach In and Put Some Color On*, voted Nonfiction Finalist of 2009 by SIBA, the SIBA Independent Booksellers Alliance, and the May 2011 sequel, *Sue Ellen's Girl Ain't Fat, She Just Weighs Heavy!,* also nominated as a SIBA Independent Booksellers Alliance Pick for Nonfiction. Comedian Jeff Foxworthy called her last book, "Laugh out loud funny!" Shellie adamantly denies bribing him for his endorsement. Her most recent release, *Heart Wide Open,* released March 2014 by Random House/Waterbrook, is enjoying an enthusiastic welcome in the faith market.

Shellie is owner, creator, and publisher of *All Things Southern*, a website updated weekly with fresh southern features. These three-minute features run each week on twenty-eight radio stations across the States as pre-taped segments comprising her daily radio show, "All Things Southern." Shellie also hosts her own talk show, ATS LIVE, every Monday evening at 5–6 PM CST on TALK 540 KMLB. One of her popular segments each week is the fifteen-minute author interview where Shellie interviews fellow authors. The show streams live, and podcasts are available so everyone can join Shellie's southern celebration!

Shellie writes a weekly inspirational feature in *Newsstar*, a Gannett paper serving Arkansas/Louisiana/Mississippi, pens a monthly print and online column for regional magazine Louisiana Road Trips, and enjoys a busy speaking schedule.

CONNECT WITH SHELLIE

Hey y'all! I love connecting with readers. You can find me on Facebook, follow me on Twitter (@shelliet), or swap pics with me on Instagram and Pinterest! Not into social media? Feel free to e-mail me (tomtom@allthingssouthern.com) or send an actual letter to 610 Schneider Lane, Lake Providence, LA 71254. Do you participate in a book club? I'd consider it a treat to connect with you and your friends. Contact me and we'll make it happen.

You're also invited to subscribe to my website allthingssouthern.com where you'll have FREE access to all my latest recipes and ramblings and find information on booking me to speak to your church group or organization. While at my site, do check out my radio program, ATS LIVE! It airs locally on TALK540 AM, streams live so you can join our weekly porch party from wherever you are, and is podcasted for your listening convenience.

Here are some of my other books you may enjoy:

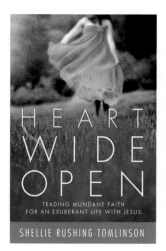
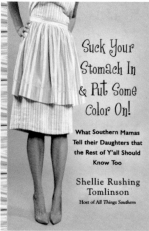

Your word-of-mouth recommendation for a book is hugely important in the publishing wheel! Would you consider reviewing *Hungry Is a Mighty Fine Sauce* on sites like Goodreads or Amazon? Many, many thanks!